Mastering Kimi AI: From Zero to Hero

A Comprehensive Technical Guide

Dr. Mohamed Refaat M. Abdellah

First Edition

2026

Copyright

This guide is provided for educational purposes. Product features, model names, pricing, APIs, and service availability may change over time. Readers should consult current official documentation before making technical or commercial decisions.

This book is independently published.

Paperback interior: 6 x 9 inches.

ISBN: 978-977-95-6874-4

First Edition: 2026

Dedication

For My parents, My Brothers

My wife "Nesreen" and my daughters: Nada, Reem and Malak

Preface

Artificial intelligence is changing how we learn, research, write, analyze information, develop software, and solve complex problems. Yet the real value of an AI system does not come from simply asking it questions. It comes from understanding its capabilities, communicating with it effectively, and applying it to meaningful tasks.

Kimi AI stands out for its ability to work with extensive context, process multiple documents and file formats, support web-assisted research, and integrate with applications through an OpenAI-compatible API. These capabilities make it valuable not only as a conversational assistant, but also as a practical tool for document analysis, research synthesis, software development, business intelligence, and workflow automation.

This book was created to provide a clear and structured path from first exposure to confident, advanced use.

Mastering Kimi AI: From Zero to Hero is organized into three progressive learning tiers. The first tier introduces Kimi AI, its architecture, its extended context window, file-processing capabilities, and the foundations of effective prompt engineering. The second tier moves into advanced interaction techniques, including long-document processing, multimodal analysis, web browsing, error handling, and response optimization. The third tier is designed for developers and technical professionals who want to use the Moonshot AI API, manage tokens and costs, build reliable applications, and apply production-ready integration strategies.

Each chapter combines explanation with practice. Learning objectives clarify what you are expected to achieve, examples demonstrate how concepts work, hands-on challenges encourage experimentation, and pro tips help you avoid common mistakes. The goal is not merely to explain features, but to help you develop repeatable methods that can be applied to real problems.

You do not need to be an AI expert to begin. Non-technical readers can progress through the foundational chapters at a comfortable pace, while developers may move directly to the integration and optimization sections after reviewing the core concepts.

Because AI platforms evolve rapidly, some interfaces, model names, limits, prices, and technical options may change after publication. The underlying principles taught in this guide—clear prompting, effective context management, careful verification, structured analysis, and responsible integration—will remain valuable even as the technology develops.

Approach the exercises with curiosity. Test different prompts, examine the results, refine your instructions, and build a personal collection of workflows that support your goals.

Your journey from zero to hero begins with a simple principle:

The quality of an AI-assisted result depends not only on the model, but also on the clarity, context, and judgment of the person using it.

— Dr. Mohamed Refaat M. Abdellah

Inside you'll find:

A Complete Learning Path from Beginner to Developer

Foundations

- A clear introduction to Kimi AI and its core architecture
- An explanation of the 200K+ context-window advantage
- Practical methods for analyzing PDFs, documents, spreadsheets, images, and code
- Prompt-engineering fundamentals for clearer and more useful responses
- A guided walkthrough of your first complete Kimi conversation

Advanced Interaction

- Advanced prompting, task decomposition, and reusable prompt patterns
- Strategies for processing long documents without losing important context
- Multimodal workflows using images, PDFs, files, and structured data
- Web browsing and real-time information-retrieval techniques
- Error-handling, troubleshooting, verification, and response optimization

Developer Integration

- Moonshot AI API architecture and authentication
- Python and cURL examples for chat-completion requests
- Message roles, parameters, response handling, and conversation management
- Token estimation, context control, and cost optimization
- Production-ready application design, monitoring, reliability, and security

- Advanced integration and performance-optimization strategies

Practical Features Throughout the Book

- Clear learning objectives
- Step-by-step technical explanations
- Real-world examples and use cases
- Ready-to-adapt prompts and code snippets
- Hands-on challenges
- Pro tips and best practices
- Checklists, quick-reference material, and tier-based appendices

Whether you are exploring AI for the first time or building intelligent applications, this guide will help you use Kimi AI with greater confidence, precision, and purpose.

About the Author

Dr. Mohamed Refaat M. Abdellah is an Associate Professor and a leading expert in software architecture, data analytics, and artificial intelligence. With over 25 years of experience, he has led numerous digital transformation initiatives and academic research projects.

He currently serves as Dean of the Education Technology Center at Misr University for Science & Technology (MUST). His work focuses on AI integration in software engineering, cybersecurity, and intelligent systems.

Dr. Abdellah holds a Ph.D. in Data Mining Security and multiple professional certifications including PMP, ITIL, and Six Sigma Black Belt.

Contents

CHAPTER 1

What Is Kimi AI? Core Concepts & Architecture

MODULE 1.1 • TIER 1: FOUNDATIONS (BEGINNER)

Learning Objective

By the end of this module, you will understand:

- What Kimi AI is and how it differs from other LLMs
- The fundamental architecture powering Kimi
- Why Kimi is uniquely positioned for long-context tasks
- Real-world use cases where Kimi excels

1.1.1 Introduction to Kimi AI

What is Kimi AI?

Kimi AI is a large language model (LLM) developed by **Moonshot AI**, a company focused on extending AI capabilities for practical applications. Unlike many mainstream models, Kimi specializes in:

- **Massive Context Windows:** 200,000+ tokens (approximately 150,000+ words in a single conversation)
- **Advanced File Understanding:** Native parsing of PDFs, documents, images, and code files
- **Web Integration:** Real-time web browsing and information retrieval
- **OpenAI-Compatible API:** Seamless integration with existing ecosystems

Why Kimi?

Imagine analyzing a 500-page technical specification, cross-referencing multiple code repositories, and asking contextual questions about the entire document without losing context. Kimi makes this possible in a single conversation.

1.1.2 How Kimi Works: Simplified Model

```
User Input
  ↓
[Tokenization Layer]
  ↓
[Context Management]
  ↓
[Neural Network Processing]
  ↓
[Attention Mechanism]
  ↓
[Output Generation]
  ↓
Response
```

Key Components

1. **Tokenization Layer:** Text broken into tokens for processing
2. **Embedding Layer:** Tokens converted to numerical representations
3. **Transformer Blocks:** Multiple layers of self-attention mechanisms
4. **Context Window:** Maintains understanding across 200K+ tokens
5. **Output Projection:** Generates human-readable text

1.1.3 Unique Selling Points

USP #1: Extended Context Window (200K+ Tokens)

- Approximately 150,000 English words
- A full-length book + detailed conversation
- Multiple code files + documentation + follow-up questions
- All in a single conversation without context loss

USP #2: Advanced File Parsing

Kimi natively understands:

- PDF documents (with OCR for scanned files)
- Code repositories (.py, .js, .java, etc.)
- Spreadsheets (.xlsx, .csv)
- Images (PNG, JPEG, SVG)
- Text files (.txt, .md, .rst)
- Office documents (.docx, .pptx)

USP #3: Web Browsing Capability

Real-time access to:

- Current news and events
- Stock prices and market data
- Latest documentation and API specs
- Scientific papers and research

USP #4: OpenAI-Compatible API

```
from openai import OpenAI

client = OpenAI(
    api_key="your_kimi_api_key",
    base_url="https://api.moonshot.cn/v1"
)
```

Your existing OpenAI code works with minimal changes!

1.1.4 Kimi vs. Traditional Search Engines

Task	Search Engine	Kimi AI
Summarize 200-page document	Manual reading (2+ hours)	Single API call (30 sec)
Compare 5 documents	Manual review (1+ hour)	Contextual analysis (1 min)
Code review with context	Fragmented results	Full codebase understanding

Task	Search Engine	Kimi AI
Conversational follow-ups	New searches needed	Seamless conversation
Real-time facts	☑ Current results	☑ With web browsing

Hands-On Challenge 1.1

Objective

Familiarize yourself with Kimi's interface and capabilities.

Challenge Steps

Step 1: Access Kimi

- Visit kimi.moonshot.cn
- Sign up for a free account
- Complete verification
- Confirm account creation

Step 2: Your First Prompt

Send this to Kimi:

```
You are an expert technical summarizer. I'll share
a document or concept with you in my next message.

Please analyze it and provide:
1. Key topics covered (3-5 bullet points)
2. Main conclusions or findings
3. Three actionable insights
4. One critical question for deeper analysis

Ready when you are!
```

Step 3: Share Your First Content

Choose one of the following:

- Paste a document excerpt (3-5 paragraphs)
- Ask about a technical concept
- Share a code snippet

- Describe a business problem

Step 4: Observation Task

As you interact, note:

- How natural does the conversation feel?
- Does Kimi ask clarifying questions?
- How specific are the recommendations?
- Does it reference your original content?
- What would a search engine do differently?

Step 5: Follow-Up Interaction

Send a clarification or follow-up question:

> "Based on your analysis, can you elaborate on the second insight? How would I apply this in a real-world scenario?"

Observe: Does Kimi maintain context from your original content?

Reflection Questions

1. **What surprised you?** About Kimi's capabilities or interaction style
2. **What was different from search?** Compared to Google or similar tools
3. **What felt natural?** What aspects of the interaction felt intuitive?
4. **What was challenging?** Did you encounter confusion or unclear results?
5. **Next use case?** What's the first real task you'd use Kimi for?

Pro Tip 1.1: Structuring Your Mental Model

Think of Kimi as a **"context-aware expert consultant"** rather than a search engine:

> ✗ Wrong: "Search for information about X"
> ☑ Right: "Given these documents, what patterns do you see across them, and what's your expert analysis?"

Key Principle: Kimi's strength lies in **contextual reasoning across large documents**, not in simple information retrieval.

Key Takeaways

- ☑ Kimi AI is a 200K+ context LLM designed for complex document analysis
- ☑ It excels at file parsing, web browsing, and extended conversations
- ☑ The OpenAI-compatible API makes integration straightforward
- ☑ It's best used as a "consultant" model rather than a search engine
- ☑ Context is king - Kimi maintains coherence across massive documents

CHAPTER 2

The 200K+ Context Window Advantage

MODULE 1.2 • TIER 1: FOUNDATIONS (BEGINNER)

Learning Objective

By the end of this module, you will understand:

- What a "context window" is and why size matters
- How 200K+ tokens translates to practical applications
- Techniques to leverage the extended context effectively
- Limitations and how to work within them

1.2.1 Understanding Context Windows

What is a Context Window?

A context window is the **maximum amount of text** (measured in tokens) that an AI model can process and maintain coherence across in a single conversation turn.

Token vs. Words: Conversion Guide

```
1 token      ≈ 4 characters
1 token      ≈ 0.75 words
1 token      ≈ 1 word (conservative estimate)

Reverse Calculations:
1 word         ≈ 1-1.33 tokens
100 words      ≈ 100-133 tokens
1,000 words  ≈ 1,000-1,333 tokens
10,000 words  ≈ 10,000-13,300 tokens
```

Real-World Token Equivalents

Token Count	English Words	Equivalent Content
1K tokens	≈ 750 words	≈ 3 pages

Token Count	English Words	Equivalent Content
5K tokens	≈ 3,750 words	≈ 15 pages
10K tokens	≈ 7,500 words	≈ 30 pages
25K tokens	≈ 18,750 words	≈ 75 pages
50K tokens	≈ 37,500 words	≈ 150 pages
100K tokens	≈ 75,000 words	≈ 300 pages
200K tokens	≈ 150,000 words	≈ 600 pages

1.2.2 Why 200K+ Matters

The Problem with Limited Context (4K-8K Tokens)

```
TURN 1: "Analyze this codebase for security issues"
     [Upload: 50KB of Python code]

AI: [Analyzes the code]
   "Found potential SQL injection..."

STATUS: Used ~3K of 4K context window
REMAINING: ~1K tokens

________________________________________

TURN 2: "What about the database layer?"

AI: "I don't have that code in context anymore.
   Please re-upload the database.py file."

✗ Problem: Context lost! Must re-upload.
```

Kimi's Advantage (200K Tokens)

```
TURN 1: "Analyze this codebase for security issues"
     [Upload: 50KB of Python code]

AI: [Analyzes the code]

STATUS: Used ~30K of 200K context window
REMAINING: ~170K tokens

________________________________________

TURN 2: "What about the database layer?
      How does it relate to the issues you found?"

AI: [References the original code]
   "Looking at how the code interacts with the database,
   the SQL injection risk is even worse..."
```

```
✅ Success: Full context maintained!
________________________________________________

TURN 3-20: Continue asking questions
        All with perfect context preservation ✅
```

1.2.3 Practical Applications

Use Case #1: Complete Code Review

You prepare and upload:

- Main application file (500 lines)
- Models file (300 lines)
- Database file (200 lines)
- Security file (150 lines)
- Tests (400 lines)
- Configuration (50 lines)
- Documentation (20 pages)

  Total: ~1,650 lines + docs = ~70K tokens

One comprehensive query:

```
Review the entire microservice for:
1. Security vulnerabilities
2. Performance bottlenecks
3. Code quality issues
4. Testing coverage gaps
5. Configuration problems

Provide specific line references for issues.
Consider interactions between modules.
```

Result: Holistic review considering all code simultaneously

Use Case #2: Research Paper Synthesis

```
You upload:
- Paper 1: Deep Learning in Medical Imaging (25 pages)
- Paper 2: Federated Learning Privacy (20 pages)
- Paper 3: Adversarial Robustness (18 pages)
- Paper 4: Model Interpretability (22 pages)

Total: 85 pages ≈ 60-70K tokens
```

```
Initial Query: "Create a synthesis document that:
1. Identifies common themes
2. Points out conflicts or differences
3. Suggests how these areas could be integrated
4. Identifies gaps in research coverage"

Result: Context-aware literature synthesis
```

Use Case #3: Business Document Analysis

```
You gather:
- Annual Report (60 pages) - 40K tokens
- Quarterly Reports (12 pages) - 8K tokens
- Board Minutes (25 pages) - 18K tokens
- Business Strategy (15 pages) - 10K tokens
- Market Analysis (20 pages) - 14K tokens
- Policies (30 pages) - 20K tokens
- Competitive Analysis (25 pages) - 17K tokens
- Industry Report (40 pages) - 28K tokens

Total: 237 pages ≈ 155K tokens

Query: "What are the top 3 strategic risks?"

Result: Analysis considering all available data
```

1.2.4 Token Counting and Management

Practical Estimation Methods

Method 1: Character Count

```
def estimate_tokens(text):
    """Quick estimation: 1 token ≈ 4 characters"""
    return len(text) // 4
```

Method 2: Word Count

```
def estimate_tokens(text):
    """More accurate: 1 token ≈ 1.33 words"""
    word_count = len(text.split())
    return int(word_count * 1.33)
```

Method 3: Professional Accuracy

```
import tiktoken

encoder = tiktoken.encoding_for_model("gpt-4")
# Kimi uses same tokenization as GPT-4

tokens = len(encoder.encode(text))
```

1.2.5 Optimal Context Usage Strategy

Strategy #1: The "Layered Document" Approach

```
Layer 1: Core Document(s)
└─ Typical allocation: 50K tokens

Layer 2: Reference Materials
└─ Typical allocation: 40K tokens

Layer 3: Previous Analysis
└─ Typical allocation: 20K tokens

Layer 4: Conversation Buffer
└─ Typical allocation: 90K tokens
```

Strategy #2: The "Question Refinement" Approach

```
Turn 1: Broad Question
├─ "What are the main issues in this codebase?"
└─ Uses: ~5K tokens (narrow response)

Turn 2: Focused Question
├─ "Deep dive into issue #3. Show me examples."
└─ Uses: ~8K tokens (detailed response)

Turn 3: Follow-up
├─ "How would you fix this issue?"
└─ Uses: ~10K tokens (comprehensive fix)

Turn 4-20: Continue Refinement
└─ Each turn adds detail and layers
```

Benefits:

- ✅ No need to re-upload documents
- ✅ Questions can reference previous answers
- ✅ Context compounds and deepens
- ✅ Natural conversational flow
- ✅ Total usage stays modest (50-60K for 20 exchanges)

Strategy #3: The "Comparative Analysis" Approach

```
Turn 1: Upload Item A
├─ Document 1: "System A Architecture" - 35K tokens
└─ Total Used: 35K | Remaining: 165K

Turn 2: Upload Item B
├─ Document 2: "System B Architecture" - 32K tokens
└─ Total Used: 67K | Remaining: 133K

Turn 3: First Comparison
```

```
├─ Query: "Compare these architectures"
└─ Response: 3K tokens | Total: 70K | Remaining: 130K

Turn 4-15: Continue Comparative Questions
└─ Each question references both documents
```

Comparative Queries:

```
☑ "How do A and B differ on point X?"
☑ "Which handles Y better and why?"
☑ "What are advantages of A vs. B?"
☑ "Can we combine the best aspects?"
☑ "Which aligns better with our goals?"
```

Hands-On Challenge 1.2

Objective

Experience the difference between limited and extended context.

Part A: Token Estimation Practice

Exercise 1: Estimate tokens for short text

```
Text: "The quick brown fox jumps over the lazy dog.
   This is a test sentence for token counting."

Step 1: Count characters
   Character count: ~102 characters

Step 2: Divide by 4
   102 ÷ 4 = ~25-26 tokens

Step 3: Count words as backup
   Words: 18 words
   Estimated tokens: 18 × 1.33 ≈ 24 tokens

Your Answer: ____ tokens (25-26 is correct)
```

Exercise 2: Estimate tokens for longer content

Find any article (500-1000 words):

```
Step 1: Count words
   Word count: _____ words

Step 2: Estimate tokens
   _____ words × 1.33 = _____ tokens

Step 3: Estimation bracket
   ☐ 600-800 tokens (small article)
   ☐ 800-1,200 tokens (medium article)
   ☐ 1,200-1,600 tokens (long article)
```

Part B: Experience Extended Context

Exercise 1: Upload and analyze a complete document

```
Step 1: Find a document (15-30 pages)
 Options:
 ☐ Research paper from arXiv.org
 ☐ Technical whitepaper
 ☐ Your company's annual report
 ☐ Product specification document
 ☐ Any PDF you have available

Step 2: Upload to Kimi
 - Open Kimi chat
 - Click "+" (upload icon)
 - Select your document
 - Wait for "Processing complete" message
 - Note the time taken: ____

Step 3: Ask Multi-Layer Questions

 Question 1 (Overview):
 "Summarize this document in 3 bullet points"

 Observation: Does Kimi capture the main points? ☐ Yes ☐ No

 Question 2 (Details):
 "What was the main research methodology?"

 Observation: Does Kimi reference specific sections? ☐ Yes ☐ No

 Question 3 (Analysis):
 "Compare the findings to common industry practice"

 Observation: Does Kimi synthesize? ☐ Yes ☐ No
 Question 4 (Application):
 "What would be the implications if we implemented this?"

 Observation: Does Kimi maintain context? ☐ Yes ☐ No
```

Pro Tip 1.2: The "Conversation Depth" Principle

Context window size directly enables **"Conversation Depth"**.

```
Small Context (4K):
Exchange 1: ■■■■ (using 1K)
Exchange 2: ■■■  (lost 1K) ✕
Exchange 3: ■■■  (lost more) ✕

Kimi 200K:
Exchange 1: ■■■■░░░░░░░░░░░░░░░░(using 5K of 200K)
Exchange 2: ■■■■■░░░░░░░░░░░░░░░░(using 10K of 200K)
Exchange 3: ■■■■■■░░░░░░░░░░░░░░░(using 15K of 200K)
...
Exchange 50: ■■■■■■■■■■■░░░░░░░░░░░░░░(using 100K of 200K) ☑
```

Practical Implication:

You can have natural, flowing conversations without constantly re-explaining your context or goals.

Key Takeaways

- ☑ Context window = Maximum tokens processable in one conversation
- ☑ 200K tokens = ~150,000 words = multiple full documents
- ☑ Prevents "context loss" after just a few exchanges
- ☑ Enables sophisticated analysis across massive documents
- ☑ Use layered strategies to maximize context efficiency
- ☑ Extended context most valuable for comparative analysis and deep dives
- ☑ Conversation depth increases dramatically with larger context windows
- ☑ Strategic token allocation enables balanced analysis and conversation

CHAPTER 3

File Parsing & Document Understanding

MODULE 1.3 • TIER 1: FOUNDATIONS (BEGINNER)

Learning Objective

By the end of this module, you will understand:

- What file types Kimi can process natively
- How Kimi extracts and understands content from files
- Best practices for uploading and organizing documents
- How to structure queries for optimal file analysis
- Troubleshooting common file parsing issues

1.3.1 Supported File Types and Formats

Category 1: Document Formats

Format	Extension	Support Level	Notes
PDF	.pdf	☆☆☆☆☆	Best support; handles scanned + digital
Word	.docx	☆☆☆☆☆	Modern format preferred
PowerPoint	.pptx	☆☆☆☆☆	Extracts text and visual context
Excel	.xlsx	☆☆☆☆☆	Reads cells, formulas, and formatting
CSV	.csv	☆☆☆☆☆	Tabular data; comma/delimiter-separated
Plain Text	.txt	☆☆☆☆☆	Universal; no formatting needed

Format	Extension	Support Level	Notes
Markdown	.md	☆☆☆☆☆	Code documentation; preserves structure

Category 2: Code and Technical Files

Language	Extensions	Support	Notes
Python	.py	☆☆☆☆☆	Full syntax understanding, PEP compliance
JavaScript	.js	☆☆☆☆☆	ES6+ syntax support
TypeScript	.ts, .tsx	☆☆☆☆☆	Full type annotation understanding
Java	.java	☆☆☆☆☆	OOP patterns recognized
C/C++	.c, .cpp, .h	☆☆☆☆☆	Systems programming patterns
SQL	.sql	☆☆☆☆☆	Multiple dialect support
HTML/CSS	.html, .css	☆☆☆☆☆	Web standards compliance
JSON	.json	☆☆☆☆☆	Structured data parsing
YAML	.yaml, .yml	☆☆☆☆☆	Configuration parsing
XML	.xml	☆☆☆☆☆	Document markup

Category 3: Data and Configuration Files

Fully Supported:

- JSON Schema files (.json)
- YAML configurations (.yaml, .yml)
- TOML configuration files (.toml)
- .env environment files
- Requirements.txt (Python dependencies)

- package.json (Node.js manifests)
- Dockerfile
- docker-compose.yml
- Kubernetes YAML (.k8s.yaml)
- Terraform files (.tf)
- CloudFormation templates (.json, .yaml)

Category 4: Images with OCR & Visual Analysis

Format	Type	Capability	Use Cases
PNG	Raster	☑ OCR + visual analysis	Diagrams, charts
JPEG	Raster	☑ OCR + visual analysis	Screenshots, photos
SVG	Vector	☑ Text extraction	Technical diagrams
GIF	Animation	☆ Frame analysis	Animated diagrams
WebP	Modern	☑ Full support	Web-optimized images

1.3.2 How Kimi Processes Files

File Processing Pipeline

```
User Uploads File
    ↓
[1] FILE VALIDATION STAGE
 ├─ Check file extension/type
 ├─ Verify file integrity
 ├─ Scan for security issues
 └─ Check size limits
    ↓
[2] CONTENT EXTRACTION STAGE
 ├─ Parse document structure
 ├─ Extract text layers
 ├─ Identify embedded objects
 ├─ Apply OCR if needed
 └─ Preserve formatting metadata
    ↓
[3] CONTEXT TOKENIZATION STAGE
 ├─ Convert content to tokens
 ├─ Maintain document structure
 ├─ Preserve section hierarchy
```

```
└─ Create searchable index
  ↓
[4] AVAILABILITY FOR ANALYSIS
├─ Content ready in conversation
├─ Full context available for queries
├─ Document metadata accessible
└─ Ready for advanced analysis
  ↓
Output: File content understood in conversation
```

PDF Processing

```
Input: filename.pdf
  ↓
Is it digital PDF (text-based)?
├─ YES: Extract text directly
│    Preserve layout information
│    Maintain heading hierarchy
│
└─ NO (Scanned/image-based):
   Apply OCR engine
   Recognize handwriting if present
   Convert images to text
   Estimate confidence levels
  ↓
Output: Full text content + metadata + OCR confidence
```

Code File Processing

```
Input: application.py
  ↓
[SYNTAX ANALYSIS]
├─ Identify language
├─ Parse code structure
├─ Recognize functions/classes
├─ Understand imports
├─ Map dependencies
  ↓
[SEMANTIC UNDERSTANDING]
├─ Map function calls
├─ Identify logic flow
├─ Understand variable scope
├─ Find potential issues
├─ Recognize design patterns
  ↓
[KNOWLEDGE INTEGRATION]
├─ Match against known libraries
├─ Identify API usage
├─ Recognize best/worst practices
└─ Compare with standards
  ↓
Output: Full code understanding + identified issues
```

1.3.3 File Upload Best Practices

Best Practice #1: Clear, Descriptive File Naming

```
✗ Bad File Names:
- "document.pdf" (Too generic)
```

- "final_final_v2.docx" (Ambiguous versions)
- "IMG_20240101_123456.jpg" (No context)
- "untitled.txt" (Not descriptive)

✅ Good File Names:
- "Q4_2024_Financial_Report.pdf"
- "SystemArchitecture_v2.3_Final.docx"
- "API_Documentation_2024.md"
- "ProductSpecification_v1.0.docx"
- "SecurityAudit_Report_Final.pdf"
- "CodeReview_ProductionAPI.py"

Best Practice #2: Organize Related Documents

❌ Inefficient: Upload 10 files separately

✅ Efficient: Organize logically
├─ Upload Core Document first (main analysis material)
├─ Upload Supporting files next (references)
└─ Reference them explicitly in your first prompt

Best Practice #3: Prepare Documents Before Upload

For Code Reviews:

- ✅ Ensure code is well-commented
- ✅ Add docstrings to functions
- ✅ Include README or documentation
- ✅ Add file structure overview
- ✅ Remove debugging code
- ✅ Verify no sensitive data

For Document Analysis:

- ✅ Use clear formatting
- ✅ Include table of contents
- ✅ Add section headers
- ✅ Number pages
- ✅ Fix obvious errors
- ✅ Include diagrams with labels

For Data Analysis:

- ✅ Clean the data (remove corruption)

- ☑ Fix obvious errors
- ☑ Include data dictionary
- ☑ Add context about dataset
- ☑ Explain column meanings
- ☑ Include units (if numerical)

Best Practice #4: File Size Considerations

File Size	Status	Recommendation
< 1MB	☑ Perfect	Upload directly
1-10MB	☑ Good	Generally fine
10-50MB	☑ Acceptable	May take 10-30 seconds
50-100MB	⚠ Large	Processing takes longer
> 100MB	✕ Too large	Consider splitting

1.3.4 Querying Uploaded Files Effectively

Query Structure for File Analysis

The most effective queries follow this structure:

```
[Context Setting] + [Specific Request] + [Output Format] = Success

FORMULA BREAKDOWN:

[Context Setting]:
├─ What is the document about?
├─ What's your role/perspective?
├─ What's the business context?
├─ What's your goal with this analysis?
└─ Who is the audience?

[Specific Request]:
├─ What exactly should Kimi analyze?
├─ What level of detail?
├─ What aspects are important?
├─ Any constraints or guidelines?
└─ Are there specific concerns?

[Output Format]:
├─ How should results be organized?
├─ What structure/format?
├─ Should it be summary or detailed?
├─ Any specific examples needed?
└─ Should results be actionable?
```

Complete Example Query

> "This PDF contains our API documentation for internal systems.
> Please identify all endpoints that handle user authentication
> and payment processing, then summarize their security best practices.
>
> Format as a table with columns:
> - Endpoint Name
> - HTTP Method
> - Authentication Type
> - Security Features
> - Potential Vulnerabilities"

Query Types and Examples

Type 1: Summarization

> Query: "This research paper discusses machine learning applications
> in healthcare. Summarize the main findings and implications
> in 5 bullet points."

Type 2: Information Extraction

> Query: "This company directory contains employee contact information.
> Extract all email addresses, phone numbers, and departments.
> Organize in a CSV-like format (name | email | phone | dept)"

Type 3: Comparison Analysis

> Query: "I've uploaded two proposals for our infrastructure upgrade.
> Compare them in terms of:
> - Cost and ROI
> - Implementation timeline
> - Technical approach
> - Risk factors
> - Resource requirements"

Type 4: Code Review

> Query: "This Python code handles user authentication.
> Review for security vulnerabilities:
> - SQL injection risks
> - Password handling
> - Session management
> - Encryption practices
>
> Provide specific line references."

Type 5: Data Analysis

> Query: "This spreadsheet contains sales data for 2024.
> Analyze for:
> - Monthly trends
> - Top performing products
> - Regional performance differences
> - Seasonal patterns
>
> Identify the most significant insights."

1.3.5 Advanced File Parsing Scenarios

Scenario 1: Multi-Document Analysis

Case: Company Security Posture Analysis

```
FILES UPLOADED:
1. SecurityPolicy.pdf (20 pages)
2. AuditReport.docx (15 pages)
3. NetworkDiagram.png
4. Incidents.csv
5. ComplianceRequirements.md

QUERY:
"Synthesize all documents. Where are our biggest
security gaps relative to our stated policies and
compliance requirements? What's our risk level?"

ANALYSIS INCLUDES:
✅ What policies require (SecurityPolicy.pdf)
✅ What audit found (AuditReport.docx)
✅ System architecture (NetworkDiagram.png)
✅ Incident history (Incidents.csv)
✅ External requirements (ComplianceRequirements.md)

RESULT:
Comprehensive security assessment with:
- Gap identification
- Risk prioritization
- Compliance status
- Recommendations
```

Scenario 2: Version Comparison

Case: API Upgrade Planning

```
FILES:
1. APIv1.0_Specification.pdf
2. APIv2.0_Specification.pdf
3. MigrationGuide.md

QUERIES:
1. "What are the breaking changes between v1.0 and v2.0?"
2. "Which of our internal services will be affected?"
3. "Create a migration plan with timeline"

RESULT:
Complete migration plan with:
✅ Breaking change list
✅ Service impact matrix
✅ Migration sequence
✅ Timeline
✅ Testing strategy
✅ Rollback plan
```

Scenario 3: Code with Complete Documentation

Case: Legacy System Understanding

```
FILES:
1. LegacyCodebase.py (500 lines)
2. SystemDesignDoc.pdf (30 pages)
3. ArchitectureNotes.txt (10 pages)
4. DatabaseSchema.sql (100 lines)
5. CodeComments_Analysis.md

QUERIES:
1. "What was the original design intent?"
2. "How has implementation diverged from design?"
3. "What's the technical debt?"
4. "Create a refactoring plan"

RESULT:
Complete understanding enabling safe refactoring
```

1.3.6 File Parsing Limitations & Solutions

Limitation #1: Very Large Directories

Challenge: Want to upload entire GitHub repo (1000+ files)

Solution 1A: Create Strategic Summary

```
Instead of uploading all 1000 files:

Step 1: Create analysis document with:
- Repository structure
- Directory tree
- Key files overview

Step 2: Upload only critical files:
- main.py (business logic)
- api.py (REST interface)
- database.py (data persistence)
- README.md (documentation)

Step 3: Query using structure context:
"Using this repository structure, analyze..."
```

Solution 1B: Extract Relevant Subset

```
Using git commands:
git log --name-only --format="" | head -50
git checkout HEAD -- src/
git archive HEAD -- src/ tests/ config/ > critical.tar
```

Limitation #2: Binary Files

Challenge: Want to analyze .exe, .dll, .so files

Solutions:

1. Use decompiler to convert to source code
2. Upload source code instead
3. Upload documentation about the binary
4. Describe binary's purpose and behavior

Limitation #3: Very Large Single File

Challenge: 500MB single log file

Solutions:

1. Split the file:

```
head -n 100000 large_log.txt > log_part1.txt
tail -n +100001 large_log.txt > log_part2.txt
```

2. Filter to relevant content
3. Create summary of issues
4. Upload processed version

Limitation #4: Corrupted Files

Challenge: File appears corrupted or incomplete

Solutions:

1. Verify file integrity
2. Re-download or recreate
3. Convert to different format
4. Try alternative download method

1.3.7 File Parsing Quality Indicators

How to Verify Kimi Understood Your File

✅ **Signs Everything Works:**

- Kimi references specific page numbers
- Quotes exact text from document
- Identifies document structure
- Mentions specific figures/data points
- Provides accurate numbers

❌ **Warning Signs:**

- Generic responses without references
- Incorrect data values
- Misses obvious information
- Can't find information you know is there

Hands-On Challenge 1.3

Objective

Master file uploading and develop effective analysis queries.

Challenge Part A: Single Document Analysis

Step 1: Find a document (10-30 pages)

- Research paper from arXiv.org
- Technical whitepaper
- Business proposal
- Product specification

Step 2: Upload to Kimi

- Click "+" (upload icon)
- Select your document
- Wait for "Processing complete"

Step 3: Craft Analysis Queries

```
QUERY 1: "Summarize this document in 5 bullet points"
Observation: Does Kimi capture main themes? ☐ Yes ☐ No

QUERY 2: "What was the main approach/methodology?"
Observation: References specific sections? ☐ Yes ☐ No

QUERY 3: "What would be the implications if we implemented this?"
Observation: Maintains document context? ☐ Yes ☐ No

QUERY 4: "For someone unfamiliar, what key concepts matter most?"
Observation: Quality of explanation? ☐ Poor ☐ Fair ☐ Excellent
```

Step 4: Count your questions

```
Total questions asked: ____
Did context loss occur? ☐ Yes ☐ No
Time for analysis: ____ minutes
```

Challenge Part B: Multi-Document Comparison

Step 1: Find two related documents

- Two research papers on similar topics
- Two versions of a proposal
- Product spec + competitor analysis
- Original design + implementation

Step 2: Upload both documents

Step 3: Ask Comparative Questions

```
QUERY 1: "What are the major differences?"
QUERY 2: "Which document makes stronger argument?"
QUERY 3: "Are there any contradictions?"
QUERY 4: "Can we combine the best aspects?"
```

Pro Tip 1.3: The "Context Sandwich" Technique

Bookend your file analysis with context:

```
[Before] → "This document is about X from Y.
    It's important because Z."
[Query] → "Analyze this for [specific request]"
[After] → "Given what we're trying to accomplish
    (project goal), what's most critical?"
```

Why it works: Gives Kimi framing for better analysis

Key Takeaways

- ☑ Kimi supports 30+ file types natively
- ☑ Advanced OCR handles scanned documents automatically
- ☑ Upload multiple files for comparative analysis
- ☑ Clear naming and organization improves quality
- ☑ Structure queries with [Context] + [Request] + [Format]
- ☑ Multi-document analysis is a major Kimi strength
- ☑ Verify parsing quality by checking specific references

CHAPTER 4

Prompt Engineering Fundamentals For Chat

MODULE 1.4 • TIER 1: FOUNDATIONS (BEGINNER)

Learning Objective

By the end of this module, you will understand:

- What prompt engineering is and why it matters
- How to write clear, specific prompts
- Techniques to structure prompts for better responses
- How to refine prompts iteratively
- Common anti-patterns to avoid

1.4.1 What is Prompt Engineering?

Definition

Prompt engineering is the art and science of crafting inputs (prompts) to AI systems to get desired outputs. It's the conversation design that makes the difference between mediocre and exceptional results.

Why Prompt Engineering Matters

```
PROMPT 1 (Poor):
"Tell me about security"

RESPONSE 1 (Generic):
"Security is important in today's digital world..."
(Vague, generic, not actionable)
```

```
PROMPT 2 (Good):

"This is my REST API. What security best practices
should I implement?"

RESPONSE 2 (Specific):
"For a REST API, prioritize:
1. HTTPS for all endpoints
2. API key authentication
3. Rate limiting
4. Input validation
5. SQL injection prevention..."
(Specific, actionable, focused)

________________________________________________

PROMPT 3 (Excellent):

"This is my REST API built with Node.js and Express
for our SaaS product with 100K daily requests. We have
~5 million daily requests and need 99.9% uptime. Our team
uses Node.js and PostgreSQL. What are the top 5 security
best practices I should prioritize?"

RESPONSE 3 (Excellent):
"For your Node.js/Express SaaS API:
1. Implement HTTPS + HSTS
2. Use bcrypt for password hashing
3. Implement rate limiting
4. Validate all input with joi
5. Use parameterized queries

Given 100K daily users, also consider:
- Caching strategy
- Graceful degradation
- Regular security audits"
(Highly specific, technology-aware, prioritized)

IMPACT:
Prompt 1 → Generic answer
Prompt 2 → Relevant answer (3x better)
Prompt 3 → Customized answer (10x better)
```

1.4.2 Anatomy of an Effective Prompt

The Essential Components

```
[CONTEXT] + [TASK] + [CONSTRAINTS] + [FORMAT] = EXCELLENT RESPONSE
```

Component 1: Context

Sets the background and helps Kimi understand the situation.

```
✅ Good Context:
"I'm a CTO at a startup building a mobile app for
fitness tracking. We have 5 developers and a budget
of $50K for infrastructure."

What it tells Kimi:
```

```
- Role: Technical decision-maker
- Industry: Fitness/SaaS
- Team size: Small (5 devs)
- Budget constraints: Limited ($50K)
- Product: Mobile app

✗ Poor Context:
"Help me with my project"

What it tells Kimi:
- Nothing. Too vague.
```

Component 2: Task

The specific action you want Kimi to perform.

```
✅ Good Task:
"Recommend a database solution for our fitness app.
Consider: read-heavy workload, real-time updates needed,
and cost efficiency."

What it tells Kimi:
- Action: Recommend (not "tell me about")
- Focus: Database solution
- Considerations: Performance, real-time, cost

✗ Poor Task:
"What's a database?"

What it tells Kimi:
- Undefined action
- Unclear scope
```

Component 3: Constraints

Limitations or specific requirements.

```
✅ Good Constraints:
"Must use open-source tools (budget constraint)
Must be learnable by junior developers
Must integrate with existing AWS infrastructure"

What it tells Kimi:
- Budget: Open-source only
- Team capability: Junior-friendly
- Technical: AWS integration required
- Implications: Rules out expensive proprietary tools

✗ Poor Constraints:
"Make it good"

What it tells Kimi:
- Undefined quality criteria
```

Component 4: Format

How you want the response structured.

```
✅ Good Format:
"Provide your recommendation as:
1. Database type (with justification)
2. Specific product recommendation
3. Estimated costs
4. Setup time and effort
5. Top 3 risks
6. Integration approach"

What it tells Kimi:
- Structure: 6 specific sections
- Level of detail: Estimates and analysis
- Actionability: Implementation considerations

✕ Poor Format:
"Just tell me what to use"

What it tells Kimi:
- No format specified
- May get prose instead of structure
```

1.4.3 The "Three-Level" Prompt Framework

Framework Overview

Create prompts at three increasing levels of sophistication:

```
LEVEL 1: BASIC
├─ What you want
└─ Simple query

LEVEL 2: STRUCTURED
├─ Context (why)
├─ Task (what)
├─ Constraints (limitations)
└─ Format (how)

LEVEL 3: OPTIMIZED
├─ Role/perspective
├─ Detailed context
├─ Specific constraints
├─ Exact format
├─ Success criteria
└─ Examples (if needed)
```

Level 1: Basic Prompts

Use when: Quick questions, simple requests, brainstorming

```
Example 1: "Summarize this article"
Example 2: "What's the best Python package for X?"
Example 3: "Help me understand decorators"

Characteristics:
- Direct and simple
- Good for quick answers
- Works when Kimi has clear context
- May need follow-ups for refinement
```

Level 2: Structured Prompts

Use when: Medium complexity, professional work, defined goals

Template:

```
"I'm [role/context]. I need to [task].
Constraints: [limitations].
Format: [desired structure]."
```

Level 3: Optimized Prompts

Use when: Complex requirements, high-stakes decisions

Template:

```
"I'm a [specific role] working on [project type].
Context: [detailed situation]

I need you to [specific task].

Constraints:
- [Technical constraints]
- [Resource constraints]
- [Organizational constraints]

Success criteria:
- [Must have 1]
- [Must have 2]
- [Nice to have]

Format: Provide [structure] with [specific details]"
```

1.4.4 Prompt Engineering Techniques

Technique 1: The "Role-Play" Approach

Assign Kimi a role to shape responses to your needs.

```
Basic: "Explain REST APIs"

Better: "Explain REST APIs as if you're teaching
    a complete beginner"

Excellent: "You're a technical interviewer testing
    a junior developer's knowledge. Explain
    REST APIs and ask 2-3 follow-up questions
    to probe their understanding."
```

Technique 2: The "Three-Part" Structure

Break complex requests into three parts:

```
PART 1: Foundation
├─ Establish basic understanding
├─ Define key concepts
└─ Set common ground

PART 2: Analysis
├─ Deep-dive into specifics
├─ Compare options
├─ Evaluate tradeoffs

PART 3: Application
├─ Apply to your situation
├─ Create actionable plan
└─ Address risks
```

Technique 3: The "Constraint-Based" Method

Explicitly state what you WON'T accept.

```
❌ Without constraints:
"Recommend a database"

✅ With constraints:
"Recommend a database.

Constraints:
- Must be open-source
- Must run on low-cost cloud instances
- Must handle time-series data
- Must not require specialist knowledge"
```

1.4.5 Common Prompt Anti-Patterns to Avoid

Anti-Pattern 1: Vagueness

```
❌ Vague:
"Analyze this code"

✅ Clear:
"Analyze this code for security vulnerabilities.
Focus on: input validation, authentication,
and data access control."
```

Anti-Pattern 2: Overloading

```
❌ Too Much:
"Read these 5 documents, summarize them, compare them,
identify gaps, create an action plan, estimate costs,
assess risks, and recommend a strategy."

✅ Chunked:
Query 1: "Summarize these 5 documents"
Query 2: "Compare them on these dimensions"
Query 3: "What gaps exist?"
Query 4: "What would you recommend and why?"
```

Anti-Pattern 3: Ambiguous Instructions

```
❌ Ambiguous:
"Make it better"

✅ Specific:
"Make this code:
- More performant (reduce database queries)
- More testable (improve function isolation)
- More readable (better variable names)"
```

Anti-Pattern 4: Lack of Context

```
❌ No Context:
"Should we use PostgreSQL or MongoDB?"

✅ With Context:
"We're building a SaaS app for real-time collaboration.
We have: 50K daily users, need <100ms latency,
team of 3 experienced SQL engineers. Budget: $5K/month.
Should we use PostgreSQL or MongoDB?"
```

1.4.6 Iterative Prompt Refinement

The Feedback Loop

```
START with Prompt
   ↓
Get Response
   ↓
Is response adequate? → YES → Done
   ↓
   NO
   ↓
Analyze what was missing/wrong
   ↓
Refine prompt
   ↓
[Loop back]
```

Refinement Strategies

Strategy 1: Add More Context

```
ITERATION 1:
"What programming language should I learn?"
Response: Generic list

ITERATION 2 (Add Context):
"I have 5 years of JavaScript experience.
I want to build backend services."
Response: More relevant

ITERATION 3 (More Details):
"I want high-performance services. My team prefers
```

compiled languages. We need heavy computational ability."
Response: Specific (Go/Rust)

Hands-On Challenge 1.4

Objective

Master prompt engineering through hands-on practice.

Challenge Part A: Prompt Quality Comparison

Step 1: Write Three Versions

Choose a topic you want to learn or a problem you want solved.

Vague Prompt (Version 1):

Vague Prompt: "Tell me about [topic]"

Send this to Kimi.
Response quality: ☐ Poor ☐ Fair ☐ Good ☐ Excellent
Notes on response: ____________________

Structured Prompt (Version 2):

Structured Prompt:
"I'm [role]. I'm interested in [topic].

Constraints:
- [your constraint 1]
- [your constraint 2]

I'd like [specific request]"

Send to Kimi.
Response quality: ☐ Poor ☐ Fair ☐ Good ☐ Excellent
Improvement from Version 1: ☐ None ☐ Slight ☐ Significant ☐ Major

Optimized Prompt (Version 3):

Optimized Prompt:
"I'm a [specific role] working on [specific project].

Context:
- [detailed background]
- [current situation]
- [constraints]
- [goals]

I need [specific task].

Constraints:
- [technical]
- [resource]
- [timeline]

```
Format: [specific structure desired]"

Send to Kimi.
Response quality: ☐ Poor ☐ Fair ☐ Good ☐ Excellent
Improvement from Version 1: ☐ 2x ☐ 5x ☐ 10x ☐ Transformational
```

Step 2: Analyze the Differences

```
Quality Metrics:
         Version 1   Version 2   Version 3
Relevance:   ☐ Low      ☐ Medium    ☐ High
Specificity: ☐ Vague    ☐ Detailed  ☐ Precise
Actionable:  ☐ No       ☐ Partially ☐ Yes
Usefulness:  ☐ Low      ☐ Medium    ☐ High
```

Pro Tip 1.4: The "Context Stack" Technique

Building up context progressively to create increasingly useful responses.

```
LEVEL 0 (No context): "Analyze this code"
Response: Generic analysis

LEVEL 1 (Who): "I'm a junior developer"
Response: Adjusted for experience

LEVEL 2 (What): "I'm building an API"
Response: API-specific

LEVEL 3 (Why): "We need to handle high traffic"
Response: Scalability-focused

LEVEL 4 (How): "Using Node.js and PostgreSQL"
Response: Tech-stack appropriate

LEVEL 5 (Constraints): "Budget is $5K/month"
Response: Cost-conscious

Result: 10x more relevant response
```

Key Takeaways

- ☑ Prompt engineering is the skill of crafting better inputs
- ☑ Effective prompts include: Context, Task, Constraints, Format
- ☑ Use the Three-Level Framework
- ☑ Role-play technique shapes responses
- ☑ Avoid vagueness, overloading, and unclear instructions
- ☑ Iterate and refine prompts for better results

- ☑ Context stacking makes responses progressively more relevant
- ☑ Specific prompts yield 5-10x better responses

CHAPTER 5

Your First Kimi Conversation: Guided Walkthrough

MODULE 1.5 • TIER 1: FOUNDATIONS (BEGINNER)

Learning Objective

By the end of this module, you will:

- Have completed your first meaningful Kimi conversation
- Understand how to structure conversation flow
- Know when to ask follow-ups vs. when to start fresh
- Be ready to use Kimi for real-world tasks

1.5.1 Pre-Conversation Checklist

Before starting your first real conversation with Kimi, ensure:

```
PREPARATION CHECKLIST:

☐ Kimi account created and logged in
☐ Know what you want to accomplish (be specific)
☐ Have any documents ready to upload (optional)
☐ Understand the 200K context window
☐ Familiar with file types Kimi supports
☐ Reviewed prompt engineering tips
☐ 20-30 minutes of uninterrupted time available

GOAL CLARITY:

What is your goal for this conversation?
☐ Learn something new
☐ Solve a specific problem
☐ Get recommendations
☐ Create something
☐ Analyze/Review content
☐ Make a decision

Write your goal in one sentence:
_______________________________
```

1.5.2 The Natural Conversation Arc

Most effective conversations follow this pattern:

```
PHASE 1: ESTABLISH CONTEXT (1 message)
├─ Set the scene
├─ Explain your role/situation
├─ State what you need
└─ Kimi demonstrates understanding

PHASE 2: INITIAL RESPONSE (1-2 messages)
├─ Kimi provides initial analysis/answer
├─ You assess if it's on the right track
└─ If yes → Phase 3; If no → clarify

PHASE 3: REFINEMENT (2-5 messages)
├─ Ask follow-up questions
├─ Provide more specific context if needed
├─ Drill into specific areas of interest
└─ Build understanding progressively

PHASE 4: APPLICATION (1-2 messages)
├─ Apply to your specific situation
├─ Get actionable next steps
├─ Address specific concerns
└─ Move toward decision/action

PHASE 5: CLOSURE (1 message)
├─ Final question or clarification
├─ Thank you / acknowledgment
└─ Conversation ends naturally

TOTAL: 6-12 messages for a productive conversation
```

1.5.3 Real Conversation Template

Use this template for your first real conversation:

```
OPENING MESSAGE:

"I'm a [your role/level] [optional: with X years experience].

Context:
- I'm [what you're working on]
- Current situation: [describe]
- Constraints: [what's limiting you]
- Goal: [what you want to achieve]

Specific need:
[What you need help with]

Format: [How you'd like the response structured, if you care]"
```

Hands-On Challenge 1.5: Your First Conversation

Objective

Complete a meaningful first conversation with Kimi

Step 1: Choose Your Topic (5 minutes)

```
I want Kimi to help me with:
☐ Learn/understand something
☐ Solve a specific problem
☐ Make a decision
☐ Create/generate something
☐ Analyze/review content
☐ Plan/strategize

Topic: ___________________
Why this matters: _______________
```

Step 2: Prepare Your Context (10 minutes)

```
MY OPENING PROMPT:

"I'm a [role] [optional: with X years experience].

Context:
[Detailed but concise situation]

Constraints:
[What's limiting your options]

I need help with:
[Specific request]

Format: [If you care how it's structured]"
```

Step 3: Open Kimi and Send (2 minutes)

```
1. Go to kimi.moonshot.cn
2. Start a new conversation
3. Paste/type your opening message
4. Send

Initial impression:
- Did Kimi understand you? ☐ Yes ☐ Partially ☐ No
- Is response on target? ☐ Yes ☐ Close ☐ Off-target
- Quality: ☐ Poor ☐ Fair ☐ Good ☐ Excellent
```

Step 4: First Follow-Up (10 minutes)

Send your first follow-up question based on Kimi's response.

Step 5: Continue for 3-5 Total Exchanges (20 minutes)

```
For each exchange:
1. Note what question you're asking
2. Rate response quality (1-10)
3. Note if Kimi maintained context
4. Decide if you need another follow-up

Continue until you have what you need.
```

Step 6: Reflection (10 minutes)

```
CONVERSATION SUMMARY:

Total exchanges: ____
Total time spent: ____ minutes
Number of follow-ups needed: ____

Quality Assessment:
- Did Kimi understand your goal? ☐ Yes ☐ Partially ☐ No
- Overall usefulness: ☐ 1-3 ☐ 4-6 ☐ 7-9 ☐ 10

What would you do differently next time?
________________________

Key takeaway:
________________________
```

Key Takeaways

- ☑ Effective conversations have clear context and goals
- ☑ Follow natural flow: Setup → Response → Refinement → Application → Closure
- ☑ Follow-up questions deepen understanding
- ☑ Context is maintained throughout conversation
- ☑ 6-12 message conversations are typically most effective
- ☑ Your opening message quality determines entire conversation value
- ☑ Specific context beats generic requests 10:1

CHAPTER 6

Advanced Prompt Engineering Techniques

MODULE 2.1 • TIER 2: ADVANCED INTERACTION (INTERMEDIATE)

Learning Objective

By the end of this module, you will understand:

- Chain-of-thought prompting and why it improves reasoning
- Few-shot and zero-shot learning patterns
- Task decomposition for complex problems
- Specialized prompt patterns for different domains
- How to detect and fix prompt failures

2.1.1 Chain-of-Thought Prompting

What is Chain-of-Thought?

Chain-of-thought (CoT) prompting asks AI to explain its reasoning step-by-step before providing an answer.

```
WITHOUT CHAIN-OF-THOUGHT:
________________________

Question: "A store has 50 red boxes and 30 blue boxes.
    If they sell 15 red boxes and buy 10 more blue boxes,
    how many total boxes do they have?"

Response: "The store has 75 total boxes."

Problem: Can't verify reasoning; answer might be wrong

WITH CHAIN-OF-THOUGHT:
______________________

Question: "A store has 50 red boxes and 30 blue boxes.
```

If they sell 15 red boxes and buy 10 more blue boxes, how many total boxes do they have?

Please show your step-by-step reasoning."

Response: "Let me work through this step-by-step:

Step 1: Starting inventory
- Red boxes: 50
- Blue boxes: 30
- Total: 80 boxes

Step 2: They sell 15 red boxes
- Red boxes: 50 - 15 = 35
- Blue boxes: 30 (unchanged)

Step 3: They buy 10 more blue boxes
- Red boxes: 35 (unchanged)
- Blue boxes: 30 + 10 = 40

Step 4: Calculate total
- Total boxes: 35 + 40 = 75 boxes

Answer: 75 total boxes"

Benefit: Clear reasoning you can verify and correct

When Chain-of-Thought Helps Most

☆☆☆☆☆ EXCELLENT USE CASES:

Complex Logic:
- Multi-step calculations
- Conditional reasoning
- Cause-and-effect analysis
- Problem-solving requiring steps

Analysis Tasks:
- Code review analysis
- Architecture assessment
- Strategy evaluation
- Risk assessment

Decision-Making:
- Choosing between options
- Weighing tradeoffs
- Evaluating pros/cons
- Recommending actions

☆☆ LESS CRITICAL:

Factual Questions:
- "What year was X invented?"
- "What does X mean?"
- "How do you spell X?"

Simple Retrieval:
- Looking up information
- Listing items
- Basic summarization

Chain-of-Thought Templates

Template 1: Simple CoT

> "[Question]
>
> Please work through this step-by-step, showing your reasoning for each step, then provide your final answer."

Template 2: Structured CoT

> "[Complex Problem]
>
> Walk me through your thinking:
> 1. What's the core question?
> 2. What information is relevant?
> 3. What are possible approaches?
> 4. What's the best approach and why?
> 5. What's the final answer?"

Template 3: Self-Critique CoT

> "Solve [problem] step-by-step.
>
> After you provide your answer, critique your reasoning:
> 1. What assumptions did you make?
> 2. Could any of these be wrong?
> 3. What would change if [alternative assumption]?
> 4. Is your final answer still correct?"

2.1.2 Few-Shot and Zero-Shot Learning

Understanding Shot Patterns

```
ZERO-SHOT: No examples
─────────────────────────
Prompt: "Classify this email as spam or not spam:
     'Click here to win $1000000 NOW!!!'"

Kimi classifies without seeing examples first.

PRO: Works immediately
CON: May misunderstand your criteria


FEW-SHOT: Multiple examples (2-5)
─────────────────────────────────────
Prompt: "Classify emails as spam or not spam.

Example 1:
Email: 'Click here to win $1000000 NOW!!!'
Classification: SPAM

Example 2:
Email: 'Your monthly statement is ready'
Classification: NOT SPAM

Example 3:
```

Email: 'LIMITED TIME OFFER - ACT NOW'
Classification: SPAM

Now classify:
Email: 'Please review the attached report'"

Kimi has clear pattern to follow.

PRO: Much more accurate
CON: Need to provide good examples

Few-Shot Template

"[Task description]

Here are examples of [correct/incorrect] [outputs]:

Example 1:
Input: [example input 1]
Output: [example output 1]
Explanation: [optional: why this is correct]

Example 2:
Input: [example input 2]
Output: [example output 2]

Example 3:
Input: [example input 3]
Output: [example output 3]

Now apply this pattern to:
Input: [new input to classify/analyze]"

Practical Few-Shot Example

"Classify code as 'Good Style' or 'Poor Style' based on readability, naming, and documentation.

Example 1:
Code:
```python
x = 5
y = x * 2
print(y)
```

Classification: POOR STYLE

Reason: Variables lack descriptive names

Example 2:

Code:

```
initial_user_count = 5
doubled_count = initial_user_count * 2
print(f"User count: {doubled_count}")
```

Classification: GOOD STYLE

Reason: Clear variable names, descriptive print

Now classify:

Code:

```
def calc(a, b):
    return a + b * 2
"""
```

2.1.3 Task Decomposition

What is Task Decomposition?

Breaking complex problems into smaller, manageable sub-tasks that are easier for Kimi to solve accurately.

```
MONOLITHIC APPROACH:
────────────────────

"Analyze our company's market position, competitive
landscape, growth opportunities, and risks. Then recommend
a 3-year strategy including pricing, positioning, product
development, and go-to-market plans. Also estimate financial
impact and identify key success metrics."

Problems:
✗ Too many topics
✗ Response will be shallow
✗ Hard to verify accuracy
✗ Difficult to refine specific areas

DECOMPOSED APPROACH:
────────────────────

Step 1: Analyze Current Position
"Analyze our current market position:
- Market size and growth rate
- Our market share
- Key strengths vs. competitors
- Recent performance trends"

[Get detailed market analysis]

Step 2: Competitive Analysis
"Given our market position, analyze:
- Who are our 3 main competitors?
- What are their strengths/weaknesses?
- How do we compare?"

[Get competitive comparison]

Step 3: Opportunity Assessment
"Given our position and competitors:
- What growth opportunities exist?
- What are the biggest risks?"

[Get opportunities and risks]
```

Step 4: Strategy Development
"Synthesizing all analysis, recommend:
- Positioning
- Product strategy
- Go-to-market approach"

Benefits:
☑ Each step is focused and thorough
☑ Can verify accuracy at each stage
☑ Can refine specific areas without redoing all
☑ Response quality is much higher
☑ More natural conversation flow

2.1.4 Specialized Prompt Patterns

Pattern 1: The Socratic Method

Kimi asks questions back to deepen your thinking.

> Prompt: "Use the Socratic method to help me think through whether to quit my job.
>
> Start by asking me clarifying questions that will help me understand my own motivations and constraints."
>
> Result: Kimi asks thoughtful questions instead of advising

Pattern 2: Rubber Duck Debugging

Explain your problem and Kimi helps you find the solution through explanation.

> Prompt: "Act as a rubber duck. I'll explain my code problem, and you ask clarifying questions that help me find the issue myself rather than solving it for me."
>
> Result: You find your own solution through guided questioning

Pattern 3: Devil's Advocate

Kimi challenges your thinking by arguing the opposite position.

> Prompt: "I've decided to use microservices for our architecture. Act as a devil's advocate and argue why this is a bad decision. Challenge my thinking."
>
> Result: You see potential downsides before committing

Pattern 4: Scenario Planning

> Prompt: "Create three scenarios:
>
> Scenario 1 (Optimistic): If everything goes well
> Scenario 2 (Realistic): Most likely outcome

Scenario 3 (Pessimistic): If things go wrong

For each, explain the path, timeline, and how to respond."

Result: Comprehensive scenario planning

Pattern 5: The Five Whys

Prompt: "I'm stuck with [problem]. Help me understand the root cause using the Five Whys method.

Ask me why, then why again for each answer, until we get to the root cause."

Result: Clear root cause identification

Hands-On Challenge 2.1

Objective

Master advanced prompt engineering techniques through practical application.

Challenge Part A: Chain-of-Thought Impact

Step 1: Problem Without CoT (5 minutes)

Choose a moderately complex problem. Ask without CoT:

PROMPT WITHOUT CoT:
"[Your problem statement]"

Send to Kimi.
Response: ______________________
Quality: ☐ 1/10 ☐ 3/10 ☐ 5/10 ☐ 7/10 ☐ 9/10 ☐ 10/10
Reasoning clarity: ☐ Unclear ☐ Some ☐ Very Clear

Step 2: Same Problem With CoT (5 minutes)

Ask with explicit chain-of-thought:

PROMPT WITH CoT:
"[Same problem]

Please work through this step-by-step:
1. [Step 1]
2. [Step 2]
3. [Step 3]

Show your reasoning for each step, then final answer."

Send to Kimi.
Response: ______________________
Quality: ☐ 1/10 ☐ 3/10 ☐ 5/10 ☐ 7/10 ☐ 9/10 ☐ 10/10
Reasoning clarity: ☐ Unclear ☐ Some ☐ Very Clear

Step 3: Compare

```
Quality improvement: ☐ None ☐ Slight ☐ Significant ☐ Major
Which would you use? ☐ Without CoT ☐ With CoT

KEY LEARNING:
Chain-of-thought helps Kimi reason about complex problems.
Use it for: Logic, analysis, decision-making
Don't need it for: Simple facts, basic summaries
```

Challenge Part B: Few-Shot Learning

Step 1: Zero-Shot (5 minutes)

```
ZERO-SHOT:
"Classify items as [Category A] or [Category B]:
1. [Item 1]
2. [Item 2]
3. [Item 3]"

Send to Kimi.
Accuracy: ____ / 3 correct
```

Step 2: Few-Shot (10 minutes)

```
FEW-SHOT:
"Classify items as [Category A] or [Category B].

Example 1:
Item: [example 1]
Classification: [Category A]

Example 2:
Item: [example 2]
Classification: [Category B]

Now classify:
1. [Item 1]
2. [Item 2]
3. [Item 3]"

Send to Kimi.
Accuracy: ____ / 3 correct
Improvement: ☐ None ☐ 1 correct ☐ 2+ correct
```

Pro Tip 2.1: The "Ladder of Abstraction" Technique

Move between abstract and concrete to improve understanding.

```
PATTERN:

Abstract: "Help me understand the concept of X"
Kimi: [High-level explanation]

Concrete: "Show me a specific example in [my domain]"
Kimi: [Specific example]

Abstract: "How does this relate to [related concept]?"
```

```
Kimi: [Comparison]

Concrete: "How would I apply this to [my specific situation]?"
Kimi: [Specific recommendation]

BENEFIT:
Moving between levels deepens understanding
and ensures relevance to your situation.
```

Key Takeaways

- ☑ Chain-of-thought prompting improves reasoning
- ☑ Few-shot learning clarifies task requirements
- ☑ Task decomposition improves depth for complex problems
- ☑ Specialized patterns enhance thinking
- ☑ Prompt failures have identifiable causes
- ☑ Iterative refinement is faster than starting over
- ☑ Different techniques for different task types

CHAPTER 7

Mastering Long-Context Document Processing

MODULE 2.2 • TIER 2: ADVANCED INTERACTION (INTERMEDIATE)

Learning Objective

By the end of this module, you will understand:

- Strategies for analyzing documents approaching 200K tokens
- How to prioritize information in long documents
- Techniques for comparative analysis of multiple large documents
- Optimization approaches for maintaining quality
- Advanced information retrieval within long contexts

2.2.1 Large Document Handling Strategy

Understanding Long-Document Challenges

```
CHALLENGE 1: Information Density
─────────────────────────────────
Problem: 100K tokens is a lot of information
Risk: Kimi might miss important details
Risk: Your questions might miss relevant context
Solution: Pre-processing and strategic questioning

CHALLENGE 2: Context Degradation
─────────────────────────────────
Problem: Very long documents are harder to process
Risk: Earlier content forgotten
Risk: Relationships between sections unclear

Solution: Hierarchical querying and synthesis

CHALLENGE 3: Extraction Efficiency
─────────────────────────────────
Problem: Not all document content is equally relevant
```

```
Risk: Wasting context on irrelevant sections
Risk: Not enough space for analysis

Solution: Strategic filtering and summarization
```

Pre-Processing Strategy

Before uploading massive documents, consider:

```
STEP 1: Assess Document Value
_______________________________________

Questions:
- Do I actually need all of this?
- How much is actually relevant to my question?
- Could a summary of 50 pages do the job?
- Are there sections I can skip?

ACTION: Create a focused subset

STEP 2: Strategic Section Extraction
_______________________________________

ALWAYS INCLUDE:
✅ Table of contents
✅ Executive summary
✅ Sections relevant to your question
✅ Key definitions and terminology
✅ Conclusions/recommendations

USUALLY SKIP:
✕ Lengthy background (if you understand context)
✕ Repetitive sections
✕ Case studies (if not applicable)
✕ Verbose introductions (if summary exists)
```

2.2.2 Hierarchical Document Querying

What is Hierarchical Querying?

Building understanding progressively from general to specific, using previous context to refine subsequent questions.

```
LEVEL 1: DOCUMENT OVERVIEW
├─ "What are the main topics?"
├─ "What's the overall purpose?"
└─ Goal: Understand document structure

LEVEL 2: SECTION ANALYSIS
├─ "What does Section X cover?"
├─ "What are key points in this section?"
└─ Goal: Understand major sections

LEVEL 3: DETAILED ANALYSIS
├─ "What specifically does [subsection] say about [topic]?"
```

```
├─ "How does [section A] relate to [section B]?"
└─ Goal: Deep understanding of relationships

LEVEL 4: APPLICATION
├─ "How does this apply to [your situation]?"
├─ "What should I do about [finding]?"
└─ Goal: Actionable insights
```

Implementation Example

```
SCENARIO: Analyzing 200-page technical specification

LEVEL 1: OVERVIEW (1-2 minutes)
─────────────────────────────────

Query 1: "What are the main sections?"
Response: [Kimi outlines sections]

Query 2: "What problem is this specification solving?"
Response: [Kimi explains purpose]

LEVEL 2: SECTION ANALYSIS (5-10 minutes)
─────────────────────────────────────────

Query 3: "Focus on the architecture section.
    What are the key components?"
Response: [Kimi details architecture]

LEVEL 3: DETAILED ANALYSIS (10-15 minutes)
──────────────────────────────────────────

Query 4: "Diving deeper into the database section:
    What are the specific performance requirements
    and how are they justified?"
Response: [Kimi provides details]

LEVEL 4: APPLICATION (5 minutes)
─────────────────────────────────

Query 5: "Given all this, what's the main thing
    we need to change in our current system?"
Response: [Kimi synthesizes and recommends]

TOTAL TIME: 20-30 minutes
QUALITY: Deep, accurate understanding
CONTEXT USED: ~100K tokens efficiently
```

2.2.3 Multi-Document Comparative Analysis

Comparing Large Documents

```
STEP 1: Upload All Documents
─────────────────────────────

Doc 1: Contract A (50K tokens)
Doc 2: Contract B (45K tokens)
Doc 3: Legal precedent (30K tokens)
Total: ~125K tokens (fits in 200K)
Remaining for discussion: ~75K tokens

STEP 2: Establish Structure
────────────────────────────

Query 1: "I've uploaded three legal documents.
    Briefly summarize what each contains."
Result: [Quick overview of all three]
```

```
STEP 3: Comparative Questions
─────────────────────────────────────

Query 2: "What are the main differences
    between Contract A and Contract B?"

Query 3: "Are there any conflicting terms?"

Query 4: "Which contract better aligns
    with the precedent?"

Query 5: "If I had to choose one contract,
    which would you recommend?"
```

2.2.4 Long-Context Query Optimization

Optimization Principle: Ask Smart Questions

```
VAGUE QUESTION:
──────────────────

Document: 500-page specification
Query: "What's important?"
Result: Generic answer; wasted context

SPECIFIC QUESTION:
─────────────────────

Document: 500-page specification
Query: "The specification mentions 'real-time sync'.
   Where is this discussed, what does it require,
   and what are the tradeoffs?"
Result: Precise answer; context well-utilized
```

Question Refinement

```
QUESTION PROGRESSION:

Initial: "What does this document require?"
├─ Too broad; response generic

Refined 1: "What are the database requirements?"
├─ More focused

Refined 2: "What specific consistency guarantees
    must the database provide?"
├─ Very specific

Refined 3: "The specification mentions 'eventual consistency'
    vs. 'strong consistency'. Which does it require?"
└─ Optimal: Specific with context hints
```

Hands-On Challenge 2.2

Objective

Master long-document processing techniques.

Challenge Part A: Document Pre-Processing

Step 1: Find a Large Document (5 minutes)

```
DOCUMENT SELECTION:

Find a document: ____ pages
Original size: ____ KB/MB

Does it have:
☐ Table of contents
☐ Executive summary
☐ Index/references
☐ Appendices
☐ Clear section headers
```

Step 2: Extract Strategic Subset (10 minutes)

```
EXTRACTION STRATEGY:

Content to include:
☐ Table of contents (page range: ____)
☐ Executive summary (page range: ____)
☐ Sections for analysis (page range: ____)
☐ Key definitions (page range: ____)
☐ Conclusions (page range: ____)

Total pages in extracted version: ____
Original pages: ____
Reduction: ____ %
```

Step 3: Upload and Compare

```
ANALYSIS 1: Upload Full Document
Time to upload: ____ seconds
Analysis quality: ☐ Poor ☐ Fair ☐ Good ☐ Excellent

ANALYSIS 2: Upload Extracted Version
Time to upload: ____ seconds
Analysis quality: ☐ Poor ☐ Fair ☐ Good ☐ Excellent

COMPARISON:
Quality difference: ☐ None ☐ Slight ☐ Significant
Was extraction worthwhile? ☐ Yes ☐ Neutral ☐ No
```

Challenge Part B: Hierarchical Querying

Step 1-4: Follow the four levels

LEVEL 1 QUERY: "What are the main topics?"
Response: ______________________

LEVEL 2 QUERY: "Focus on most relevant section.
What are the key points?"
Response: ______________________

LEVEL 3 QUERY: "What specifically about [subtopic]?"
Response: ______________________

LEVEL 4 QUERY: "How does this apply to my situation?"
Response: ______________________

Total time: ____ minutes
Quality: ☐ 1-3/10 ☐ 4-6/10 ☐ 7-10/10

Key Takeaways

- ☑ Large documents need strategic pre-processing
- ☑ Hierarchical querying builds understanding progressively
- ☑ Multi-document analysis benefits from all-in context
- ☑ Smart questions maximize context utility
- ☑ Citation requests ensure accuracy
- ☑ Quality verification is essential
- ☑ Performance optimization saves time and tokens

CHAPTER 8

Multimodal Inputs - Images, PDFs, And Files

MODULE 2.3 • TIER 2: ADVANCED INTERACTION (INTERMEDIATE)

Learning Objective

By the end of this module, you will understand:

- How to work with images alongside text
- Best practices for multimodal analysis
- Visual reasoning capabilities and limitations
- How to optimize mixed-format inputs
- Real-world multimodal use cases

2.3.1 Working with Images

What Kimi Can Do with Images

> ✅ READ TEXT FROM IMAGES:
> - Screenshots of websites
> - Photographs of documents
> - Scanned pages
> - Text overlaid on graphics
>
> ✅ ANALYZE VISUAL CONTENT:
> - Diagrams and flowcharts
> - Charts and graphs
> - Photographs
> - Icons and symbols
> - Layout and design
>
> ✅ INTERPRET MEANING:
> - What does this diagram show?
> - What's the relationship between elements?
> - What's the data pattern in this chart?
> - What does this design communicate?
>
> ⚠ LIMITATIONS:
> - Can't analyze videos (only images)

```
- Quality depends on image clarity
- May misinterpret complex diagrams
- Handwriting recognition limited
```

Optimal Image Formats

```
☆☆☆☆☆ EXCELLENT:
- High-quality PNG/JPEG
- Professional diagrams
- Clear screenshots
- High-resolution scans

☆☆☆☆ GOOD:
- Decent resolution images
- Most photographs
- Most documents
- Most diagrams

☆☆☆ FAIR:
- Lower resolution images
- Compressed JPEGs
- Blurry or small text
- Complex handwriting

☆☆ POOR:
- Very low resolution
- Illegible text
- Severely compressed
- Poor lighting
```

2.3.2 Multimodal Analysis Patterns

Pattern 1: Text + Image Interpretation

```
SCENARIO: Architecture diagram with documentation

INPUT:
- Document: SystemArchitecture.pdf (50K tokens)
- Image: system_diagram.png

QUERY 1: "Are the document descriptions consistent
    with what the diagram shows?"

RESPONSE: [Kimi cross-references]

QUERY 2: "What components are shown in the diagram
    but not detailed in the document?"

RESPONSE: [Kimi identifies gaps]

BENEFIT: Visual + textual understanding
```

Pattern 2: Data Visualization Analysis

```
SCENARIO: Analyzing charts and graphs

INPUT:
- Chart: sales_by_region.jpg
```

```
- Numbers: sales_data.csv

QUERY: "What patterns do you see?
    Are there anomalies?
    What's your interpretation?"

RESPONSE: [Kimi analyzes visual + data]

BENEFIT: Spot patterns humans might miss
```

Pattern 3: Multi-Image Comparison

```
SCENARIO: Before/After analysis

INPUT:
- Image 1: design_v1.png (before)
- Image 2: design_v2.png (after)

QUERY: "Compare these two designs.
    What changed?
    Is it an improvement?"

RESPONSE: [Kimi details changes]

BENEFIT: Objective comparison
```

Hands-On Challenge 2.3

Objective

Master multimodal analysis with images and documents.

Challenge Part A: Text from Image Extraction

Step 1: Prepare an Image (5 minutes)

```
IMAGE SELECTION:

Find or create an image with text:
☐ Screenshot of a website
☐ Photograph of a document
☐ Scanned page
☐ Chart with labels
☐ Diagram with text

Image quality: ☐ High ☐ Medium ☐ Low

Upload to Kimi.
```

Step 2: Extract Text (3 minutes)

```
QUERY: "What text does this image contain?
    Extract it exactly as shown."

Response: _______________
```

```
Compare to original:
Accuracy: ☐ Perfect ☐ 95%+ ☐ 80%+ ☐ <80%
```

Challenge Part B: Visual Content Analysis

Step 1: Prepare Visual Content (5 minutes)

```
VISUAL SELECTION:

Find or create:
☐ Flowchart/diagram
☐ Chart/graph
☐ Photograph/design
☐ Interface screenshot
☐ Architecture diagram

Upload to Kimi.
```

Step 2: Analyze Visually (5 minutes)

```
QUERY 1: "What does this image show?"
Response: _______________
Accurate: ☐ Yes ☐ Partially ☐ No

QUERY 2: "What are the key elements shown?"
Response: _______________
Comprehensive: ☐ Yes ☐ Somewhat ☐ No

QUERY 3: "What would you change or improve?"
Response: _______________
Quality: ☐ Shallow ☐ Medium ☐ Deep
```

Key Takeaways

- ☑ Kimi can read text from images with high accuracy
- ☑ Visual reasoning works well for moderate complexity
- ☑ Multimodal analysis combines different perspectives
- ☑ Mixed formats should have clear relationships
- ☑ Image quality directly impacts analysis quality

CHAPTER 9

Web Browsing & Real-Time Information Retrieval

MODULE 2.4 • TIER 2: ADVANCED INTERACTION (INTERMEDIATE)

Learning Objective

By the end of this module, you will understand:

- When and how to enable web browsing
- Effective queries for web-based research
- Fact-checking and verification techniques
- Combining real-time data with documents
- Limitations and appropriate use cases

2.4.1 Enabling and Using Web Browsing

When to Use Web Browsing

```
USE WEB BROWSING WHEN:

✅ You need current information
  - Stock prices, exchange rates
  - Current news, events
  - Latest research papers
  - Updated documentation
  - Real-time metrics

✅ You need information beyond training data
  - Recent announcements
  - Breaking news
  - New company information
  - Recent developments

✅ You need to verify information
  - Fact-checking claims
  - Confirming data
  - Cross-referencing sources

DON'T NEED WEB BROWSING WHEN:
```

✗ Historical information (already in training)
✗ Foundational knowledge (no need to refresh)
✗ Problem is local to you
✗ Sensitive/restricted content

How to Request Web Browsing

```
EXPLICIT REQUEST:

"Please search the web for information about [topic].
Focus on: [specific aspects]
Find: [type of information needed]"

Kimi will:
✅ Search the web
✅ Find relevant results
✅ Synthesize information
✅ Cite sources

IMPLICIT REQUEST:

"What's the current price of [stock]?"
or
"What happened with [recent event]?"

Kimi recognizes need and does it automatically.
```

2.4.2 Effective Web Research Queries

Query Patterns for Web Research

Pattern 1: Current Events Research

```
QUERY: "What are the latest developments in
    [industry/topic] in the last [timeframe]?
    Focus on: [specific aspects]"

Example:
"What are the latest developments in AI regulation
in the last 3 months?
Focus on: US, EU, and China policy changes."

Kimi will:
✅ Search for recent news
✅ Summarize developments
✅ Cite sources with dates
```

Pattern 2: Real-Time Data Queries

```
QUERY: "What is the current [metric]?
    How does it compare to [timeframe]?"

Examples:
"What is the current price of Bitcoin?"
"What is the current US unemployment rate?"
```

```
Kimi will:
☑ Find current data
☑ Provide historical comparison
```

Pattern 3: Fact-Checking

```
QUERY: "Is it true that [claim]?
    Find recent evidence/sources."

Example:
"Is it true that remote work productivity increases?
Find recent research and evidence."

Kimi will:
☑ Search for relevant research
☑ Evaluate claim
☑ Cite evidence
```

2.4.3 Combining Web Search with Documents

Integration Patterns

Pattern 1: Document + Web Context

```
SCENARIO: You have internal document, need external context

INPUT:
- Document: our_product_strategy.pdf (30K tokens)
- Web search enabled

QUERY: "We're planning [strategy from document].
    What's the current market landscape for this?
    Are there new competitors or technologies?"

RESULT:
Kimi combines:
☑ Your strategy (from document)
☑ Current market (from web)
☑ Competitive analysis (from web)
☑ Recommendations considering both
```

Hands-On Challenge 2.4

Objective

Master web-enabled research and fact-checking with Kimi.

Challenge Part A: Current Information Research

Step 1: Choose a Topic (5 minutes)

```
TOPIC SELECTION:

Choose something requiring current information:
☐ Technology news
☐ Market data
☐ Company news
☐ Industry trends
☐ Recent research

Topic: _______________
Why web search is needed: _____________
```

Step 2: Request Web Research (5 minutes)

```
QUERY: "Research [topic].
    Find current information about: [specifics]
    Sources should be from the last [timeframe]"

Send to Kimi with web browsing enabled.

Information found: ____ key points
Sources provided: ☐ Yes ☐ No
Recency: ☐ Current ☐ Recent ☐ Dated
```

Step 3: Evaluate Results (5 minutes)

```
EVALUATION:

Information quality: ☐ Poor ☐ Fair ☐ Good ☐ Excellent
Source credibility: ☐ Low ☐ Medium ☐ High

Would you trust this for decision-making?
☐ No, need more verification
☐ Maybe, with additional sources
☐ Yes, seems reliable
```

Key Takeaways

- ☑ Web browsing adds current information to Kimi's knowledge
- ☑ Appropriate for recent developments and real-time data
- ☑ Useful for fact-checking against sources
- ☑ Can combine with documents for richer analysis
- ☑ Source evaluation is critical for verification
- ☑ Web browsing has limitations
- ☑ Responsibility for ethical use rests with you
- ☑ Multiple sources provide better confidence

CHAPTER 10

Error Handling & Optimization Strategies

MODULE 2.5 • TIER 2: ADVANCED INTERACTION (INTERMEDIATE)

Learning Objective

By the end of this module, you will understand:

- Common types of errors and how to prevent them
- Detecting when Kimi is wrong
- Optimization techniques for better quality
- Debugging failed conversations
- Building confidence in results

2.5.1 Common Error Types

Error Type 1: Hallucination

Kimi generates plausible-sounding but false information.

```
HALLUCINATION EXAMPLE:

Query: "What's the current price of Bitcoin?"
(Without web search enabled)

Kimi: "Bitcoin is currently trading at $47,200"
(This could be outdated, partially made up, or wrong)

DETECTION:
- Cross-reference with authoritative source
- Check date relevance
- Verify with multiple sources

PREVENTION:
- Enable web search for current information
- Be skeptical of specific numbers
- Ask for sources
- Verify important facts
```

Error Type 2: Context Misunderstanding

Kimi misinterprets the situation or goal.

```
EXAMPLE:

You: "How do I optimize my database?"
  (For a startup with limited budget)

Kimi: "Use enterprise solutions like Oracle"
  (Completely misses budget constraint)

DETECTION:
- Response doesn't match your constraints
- Recommendations seem misaligned
- Answer seems generic

PREVENTION:
- Explicitly state constraints upfront
- Give specific examples of your situation
- Ask Kimi to confirm understanding
```

Error Type 3: Outdated Information

Using information from training data that's no longer current.

```
EXAMPLE:

Query: "What's the latest Python version?"
Kimi: "Python 3.10 is the latest"
  (Training data old; 3.13 is actually latest)

PREVENTION:
- Use web search for anything time-sensitive
- Specify desired timeframe
- Check against authoritative sources
```

Error Type 4: Over-Generalization

Applying general principles to situations where they don't apply.

```
EXAMPLE:

Kimi: "Yes, microservices are the best practice"
  (Ignores your specific constraints)

PREVENTION:
- Stress your unique constraints
- Ask "given X, Y, Z constraints..."
- Ask for caveats
```

Error Type 5: Code Errors

Generated code has bugs or incorrect syntax.

EXAMPLE:

Kimi: [Generates code with incorrect syntax]

PREVENTION:
- Test all generated code
- Ask for explanation of each step
- Request unit tests alongside code
- Verify approach before code

2.5.2 Detecting When Kimi Is Wrong

Warning Signs

⚠ SIGN 1: Over-Confident Answer

- Absolute statements
- No caveats mentioned
- No acknowledgment of complexity

What to do:
"Under what conditions might this NOT be true?"

⚠ SIGN 2: Vague or Generic Answer

- Generic statements that apply broadly
- Lack of specific examples
- Seems like boilerplate

What to do:
"This is too generic for my situation"

⚠ SIGN 3: Inconsistent with Your Knowledge

- Contradicts something you know true
- Seems to misunderstand your domain
- Advice doesn't match your experience

What to do:
"Actually, in our case, X is true because..."

⚠ SIGN 4: No Sources or Justification

- Claims without backing
- No explanation of reasoning
- No sources cited

What to do:
"Where does this come from?"

⚠ SIGN 5: Response Avoidance

- Doesn't directly answer your question
- Changes subject subtly
- Gives related but different answer

What to do:
"You haven't addressed..."
"Please clarify your question"

2.5.3 Optimization Strategies

Strategy 1: Iterative Refinement

```
CYCLE 1: Initial Response
├─ Ask question
├─ Get response
└─ Assess quality

CYCLE 2: Refinement
├─ Ask follow-up
├─ Get refined response
└─ Assess improvement

CYCLE 3+: Continued Refinement
└─ Dig deeper on weak areas
```

Strategy 2: Cross-Verification

```
TECHNIQUE:

STEP 1: Get answer from Kimi
Query: [Your question]
Response: [Answer 1]

STEP 2: Ask differently
Query: "Approach this from another angle"
Response: [Answer 2]

STEP 3: Compare
If Answer 1 ≈ Answer 2: Likely correct ✅
If Answer 1 ≠ Answer 2: Need investigation ⚠
```

Strategy 3: Explanation-Based Verification

```
Instead of just:
"Recommend a solution for X"

Ask for process:
"Walk me through your thinking:
1. What are the key considerations?
2. What are the trade-offs?
3. What's the best option and why?"
```

Hands-On Challenge 2.5

Objective

Develop error detection and correction skills.

Challenge Part A: Error Detection

Step 1: Identify Common Errors (10 minutes)

For each error type, generate a scenario:

```
SCENARIO 1 - HALLUCINATION:

Create a query likely to produce made-up info:
"[Query likely to hallucinate]"

Send to Kimi.
Response: _______________

Does it contain fabrications?
☐ Clearly ☐ Possibly ☐ Probably not

How did you detect it?
_______________________

How would you prevent it?
☐ Enable web search
☐ Request sources
☐ Ask for verification
☐ Use different approach
```

Step 2: Test Context Misunderstanding

```
QUERY WITHOUT CONTEXT:
"[Vague question without constraints]"

Kimi responds: _______________
Quality: ☐ Great ☐ Okay ☐ Off-target

NOW WITH FULL CONTEXT:
"I'm [role]. I have [constraints].
The challenge is [specific problem].
Given all this: [question]"

Kimi responds: _______________
Quality: ☐ Much better ☐ Somewhat better ☐ Same
```

Pro Tip 2.5: The "Confidence Confidence" Technique

Meta-evaluate Kimi's confidence level.

```
PATTERN:

When Kimi gives answer:

LEVEL 1: Note Kimi's apparent confidence
- Certain/confident language
- Tentative/uncertain language

LEVEL 2: Assess if confidence is justified
"How confident should someone be in this answer?"

Kimi response helps you understand:
```

```
- Is Kimi's confidence warranted?
- What would strengthen confidence?
- What would weaken confidence?

LEVEL 3: Make your own assessment
- Is Kimi's confidence appropriate?
- What additional verification do you need?

BENEFIT:
Helps you calibrate trust
Identifies when to dig deeper
Prevents over-confidence in wrong answers
```

Key Takeaways

- ☑ Hallucination is common; requires verification
- ☑ Context misunderstanding often signals weak input
- ☑ Outdated information needs web search
- ☑ Warning signs indicate when to be skeptical
- ☑ Iterative refinement improves quality
- ☑ Cross-verification builds confidence
- ☑ Explanation-based checking catches reasoning errors
- ☑ Learn from failures to improve future prompts
- ☑ Confidence assessment is part of evaluation
- ☑ Verify with authoritative sources when in doubt

CHAPTER 11

Moonshot AI API Architecture & Authentication

MODULE 3.1 • TIER 3: DEVELOPER INTEGRATION (ADVANCED)

Learning Objective

By the end of this module, you will understand:

- Moonshot AI's API structure and design
- How to authenticate with API keys securely
- Rate limits and quota management
- API endpoints and their purposes
- Best practices for API integration

3.1.1 Understanding the Moonshot AI API

API Overview

The Moonshot AI API is designed to be OpenAI-compatible, meaning it follows the same interface standards as OpenAI's API. This allows existing code to work with minimal changes.

```
MOONSHOT AI API ENDPOINTS:

Chat Completions (Primary):
└─ https://api.moonshot.cn/v1/chat/completions

Model Listing:
└─ https://api.moonshot.cn/v1/models

Models Available:
├─ kimi-k1.5 (Latest, recommended)
├─ kimi-k1 (Previous generation)
└─ Other variants as released
```

API Architecture

```
┌─────────────────────────────────────┐
│ Your Application                    │
├─────────────────────────────────────┤
│ Kimi SDK / HTTP Client              │
├─────────────────────────────────────┤
│ https://api.moonshot.cn/v1          │
├─────────────────────────────────────┤
│ Moonshot AI Infrastructure          │
├─────────────────────────────────────┤
│ Kimi AI Model                       │
└─────────────────────────────────────┘
```

3.1.2 Authentication & API Key Management

Getting Your API Key

```
STEP 1: Create Account
├─ Go to moonshot.cn or kimi.moonshot.cn
├─ Sign up with email
├─ Verify email
└─ Create account

STEP 2: Access API Dashboard
├─ Log in to account
├─ Navigate to API section
├─ Go to "API Keys" or "Keys Management"
└─ Click "Create New Key"

STEP 3: Generate API Key
├─ Provide key name (for reference)
├─ Set permissions (usually "all")
├─ Confirm generation
└─ Copy key immediately (only shown once)

STEP 4: Secure Storage
├─ Never commit to version control
├─ Use environment variables
├─ Store in .env file
├─ Use secret management systems
└─ Rotate keys periodically
```

Setting Up Authentication in Code

Python Example:

```
import os
from openai import OpenAI

# Method 1: Environment Variable (Recommended)
# Set: export MOONSHOT_API_KEY="your_api_key"
client = OpenAI(
    api_key=os.getenv("MOONSHOT_API_KEY"),
    base_url="https://api.moonshot.cn/v1"
)

# Method 2: Direct (Not Recommended for Production)
```

```
client = OpenAI(
  api_key="sk-xxxxx...",
  base_url="https://api.moonshot.cn/v1"
)

# Method 3: Using OpenAI Environment Variable
# Set: export OPENAI_API_KEY="your_api_key"
# (Works because Kimi is OpenAI-compatible)
client = OpenAI(base_url="https://api.moonshot.cn/v1")
```

Node.js Example:

```
import OpenAI from "openai";

const client = new OpenAI({
 apiKey: process.env.MOONSHOT_API_KEY,
 baseURL: "https://api.moonshot.cn/v1"
});
```

cURL Example:

```
curl -X POST https://api.moonshot.cn/v1/chat/completions \
 -H "Authorization: Bearer your_api_key" \
 -H "Content-Type: application/json" \
 -d '{
  "model": "kimi-k1.5",
  "messages": [
   {"role": "user", "content": "Hello!"}
  ]
 }'
```

API Key Security Best Practices

```
✅ DO:

☑ Store in environment variables
 export MOONSHOT_API_KEY="sk-..."

☑ Use .env file (with git ignore)
 .env file: MOONSHOT_API_KEY=sk-...
 .gitignore: .env

☑ Use secret management systems
 - AWS Secrets Manager
 - Google Cloud Secret Manager
 - HashiCorp Vault
 - GitHub Secrets

☑ Rotate keys periodically
 - Delete old keys
 - Generate new keys
 - Update all applications

☑ Use key with limited permissions
 - Only needed scope
 - Read-only if possible

✖ DON'T:

✗ Hardcode API keys in source code
✗ Commit API keys to version control
✗ Share API keys via email or messaging
```

```
✗ Use same key across multiple projects
✗ Log API keys in output
✗ Include in client-side code
```

3.1.3 Rate Limits and Quotas

Understanding Rate Limits

```
RATE LIMITS:

Requests Per Minute (RPM):
├─ Free tier: 60 RPM
├─ Standard: 200+ RPM
└─ Enterprise: Custom

Tokens Per Minute (TPM):
├─ Free tier: 100,000 TPM
├─ Standard: 1,000,000+ TPM
└─ Enterprise: Custom

Concurrent Requests:
├─ Free tier: 5 concurrent
├─ Standard: 10 concurrent
└─ Enterprise: Custom
```

Handling Rate Limits

Python with Exponential Backoff:

```
import time
import random
from openai import RateLimitError

def call_with_retry(client, **kwargs):
    max_retries = 3
    base_wait = 1

    for attempt in range(max_retries):
        try:
            return client.chat.completions.create(**kwargs)
        except RateLimitError as e:
            if attempt < max_retries - 1:
                wait_time = base_wait * (2 ** attempt)
                # Add jitter
                wait_time += random.uniform(0, 1)
                print(f"Rate limited. Waiting {wait_time:.2f}s...")
                time.sleep(wait_time)
            else:
                raise

# Usage
response = call_with_retry(
    client,
    model="kimi-k1.5",
    messages=[{"role": "user", "content": "Hello"}]
)
```

Monitoring Usage

````
TRACKING TOKENS:

In Response:
```python
response = client.chat.completions.create(...)

# Token usage information
print(f"Input tokens: {response.usage.prompt_tokens}")
print(f"Output tokens: {response.usage.completion_tokens}")
print(f"Total: {response.usage.total_tokens}")
````

Logging:

````
def log_usage(response, cost_per_input=0.0006, cost_per_output=0.0018):
    prompt_tokens = response.usage.prompt_tokens
    completion_tokens = response.usage.completion_tokens

    cost = (prompt_tokens * cost_per_input +
            completion_tokens * cost_per_output) / 1000000

    print(f"Tokens: {prompt_tokens} + {completion_tokens}")
    print(f"Cost: ${cost:.6f}")

    return cost


---

## 3.1.4 API Status and Health Checks

### Checking API Status

```python
def check_api_health(client):
    try:
        # Try listing models as a health check
        models = client.models.list()
        print("API is healthy")
        print(f"Available models: {[m.id for m in models.data]}")
        return True
    except Exception as e:
        print(f"API health check failed: {e}")
        return False

# Check before making requests
if not check_api_health(client):
    # Handle API being down
    print("API is unavailable")
````

Hands-On Challenge 3.1

Objective

Set up Moonshot API authentication and verify connectivity.

Challenge Part A: API Key Setup

Step 1: Create API Key

```
☐ Go to moonshot account
☐ Navigate to API Keys section
☐ Create new API key
☐ Copy the key immediately
☐ Store in .env file

Key created: ☐ Yes ☐ No
```

Step 2: Set Up Environment

```
Python:
Create .env file:
MOONSHOT_API_KEY=sk_test_xxxxx

Create venv:
python -m venv venv
source venv/bin/activate  # or venv\Scripts\activate on Windows

Install package:
pip install openai

JavaScript:
Create .env file:
MOONSHOT_API_KEY=sk_test_xxxxx

Install package:
npm install openai

Create .gitignore:
.env
node_modules/
```

Challenge Part B: First API Call

Python:

```
import os
from openai import OpenAI

# Setup
client = OpenAI(
    api_key=os.getenv("MOONSHOT_API_KEY"),
    base_url="https://api.moonshot.cn/v1"
)

# Make request
response = client.chat.completions.create(
    model="kimi-k1.5",
    messages=[
        {"role": "user", "content": "Say hello!"}
    ]
)

print(response.choices[0].message.content)
print(f"Tokens used: {response.usage.total_tokens}")
```

JavaScript:

```
import OpenAI from "openai";

const client = new OpenAI({
  apiKey: process.env.MOONSHOT_API_KEY,
  baseURL: "https://api.moonshot.cn/v1"
});

const response = await client.chat.completions.create({
  model: "kimi-k1.5",
  messages: [
    { role: "user", content: "Say hello!" }
  ]
});

console.log(response.choices[0].message.content);
console.log(`Tokens used: ${response.usage.total_tokens}`);
```

Challenge Part C: Verify Authentication

```
☐ Can connect to API
☐ Can make successful request
☐ Receive valid response
☐ Token count returned
☐ No authentication errors

Test Results:
Response: _______________
Status: ☐ Success ☐ Failed

If failed, check:
☐ API key is correct
☐ API key is not expired
☐ Environment variable is set
☐ Network connectivity
☐ API endpoint URL is correct
```

Key Takeaways

- ✅ Moonshot API is OpenAI-compatible
- ✅ API keys must be kept secure
- ✅ Use environment variables for storing keys
- ✅ Rate limits depend on account tier
- ✅ Implement retry logic for reliability
- ✅ Monitor token usage for cost tracking
- ✅ Always handle authentication errors

CHAPTER 12

Chat Completions API Deep Dive

MODULE 3.2 • TIER 3: DEVELOPER INTEGRATION (ADVANCED)

Learning Objective

By the end of this module, you will understand:

- The Chat Completions API request/response structure
- How to format messages correctly
- Streaming responses for real-time output
- Model selection and parameters
- Error handling and validation

3.2.1 Request Structure

Basic Request Format

```
response = client.chat.completions.create(
  model="kimi-k1.5",
  messages=[
    {"role": "system", "content": "You are a helpful assistant."},
    {"role": "user", "content": "What is 2+2?"},
    {"role": "assistant", "content": "2+2 equals 4."},
    {"role": "user", "content": "What about 3+3?"}
  ],
  temperature=0.7,
  max_tokens=2000,
  top_p=1.0
)
```

Message Structure

```
Message Object:
{
  "role": "user" | "assistant" | "system",
  "content": "Text content here",
  "name": "optional_name"  // Optional, for clarity
}

Roles:
├─ system: Instructions for Kimi's behavior
```

```
├─ user: User input/questions
└─ assistant: Previous Kimi responses

Conversation Flow:
user message
  ↓
assistant response
  ↓
user message
  ↓
assistant response
  ↓
(and so on...)
```

Request Parameters

```
REQUIRED:
- model: "kimi-k1.5" (or other available models)
- messages: List of message objects

OPTIONAL:
- temperature: 0.0-2.0 (default 0.7)
  * 0.0: Deterministic/focused
  * 1.0: Balanced
  * 2.0: Creative/random

- top_p: 0.0-1.0 (default 1.0)
  * Lower = More focused
  * 1.0 = Disabled (uses temperature)

- max_tokens: Integer (default varies)
  * Maximum output length
  * Counts only output, not input

- frequency_penalty: -2.0 to 2.0 (default 0.0)
  * > 0: Penalizes repetition
  * < 0: Encourages repetition

- presence_penalty: -2.0 to 2.0 (default 0.0)
  * > 0: Promotes new topics
  * < 0: Focuses on current topics

- stop: String or array of strings
  * Stop generation at these sequences

- user: String (optional)
  * User identifier for tracking/safety
```

3.2.2 Response Structure

Response Format

```
{
  "id": "chatcmpl-xxxxx",
  "object": "chat.completion",
  "created": 1234567890,
  "model": "kimi-k1.5",
  "choices": [
    {
      "index": 0,
```

```
        "message": {
          "role": "assistant",
          "content": "The response text here"
        },
        "finish_reason": "stop",
        "logprobs": null
      }
    ],
    "usage": {
      "prompt_tokens": 100,
      "completion_tokens": 50,
      "total_tokens": 150
    }
}
```

Extracting Response

```
# Get the response text
response_text = response.choices[0].message.content

# Check finish reason
finish_reason = response.choices[0].finish_reason
# "stop": Natural completion
# "length": max_tokens reached
# "content_filter": Blocked for safety

# Get token usage
prompt_tokens = response.usage.prompt_tokens
completion_tokens = response.usage.completion_tokens
total_tokens = response.usage.total_tokens
```

3.2.3 Streaming Responses

Why Use Streaming?

```
Non-Streaming:
└─ Wait for entire response before outputting
└─ Better for final results
└─ Full token count available immediately

Streaming:
└─ Output tokens as generated
└─ Better user experience
└─ Can start processing partial responses
└─ Real-time feel
```

Implementing Streaming

Python:

```
response = client.chat.completions.create(
    model="kimi-k1.5",
    messages=[
        {"role": "user", "content": "Write a short poem"}
    ],
    stream=True
)
```

```
# Process stream
full_response = ""
for chunk in response:
    if chunk.choices[0].delta.content:
        content = chunk.choices[0].delta.content
        print(content, end="", flush=True)
        full_response += content

print()  # Newline at end
```

JavaScript:

```
const response = await client.chat.completions.create({
  model: "kimi-k1.5",
  messages: [
    { role: "user", content: "Write a short poem" }
  ],
  stream: true
});

let fullResponse = "";

for await (const chunk of response) {
  if (chunk.choices[0].delta.content) {
    const content = chunk.choices[0].delta.content;
    process.stdout.write(content);
    fullResponse += content;
  }
}

console.log(); // Newline at end
```

3.2.4 Handling Different Response Types

Long Responses

```
# For responses that might exceed max_tokens
response = client.chat.completions.create(
    model="kimi-k1.5",
    messages=[{"role": "user", "content": "Write a 5000 word essay"}],
    max_tokens=2000  # Set reasonable limit
)

# Check if response was truncated
if response.choices[0].finish_reason == "length":
    print("Response was truncated. Consider:")
    print("1. Increase max_tokens")
    print("2. Ask for summary instead")
    print("3. Break into multiple requests")
```

Handling Errors

```
from openai import (
    APIError,
    APIConnectionError,
    RateLimitError,
    AuthenticationError
)

try:
```

```
  response = client.chat.completions.create(
    model="kimi-k1.5",
    messages=[{"role": "user", "content": "Hello"}]
  )
except AuthenticationError:
  print("API key is invalid")
except RateLimitError:
  print("Rate limit exceeded")
except APIConnectionError:
  print("Connection error to API")
except APIError as e:
  print(f"API error: {e}")
```

Hands-On Challenge 3.2

Objective

Master Chat Completions API usage.

Challenge Part A: Basic Request

Step 1: Simple Request

```
response = client.chat.completions.create(
  model="kimi-k1.5",
  messages=[
    {"role": "system", "content": "You are a helpful assistant."},
    {"role": "user", "content": "What is machine learning?"}
  ]
)

# Extract and display
print("Response:")
print(response.choices[0].message.content)
print(f"\nTokens used: {response.usage.total_tokens}")
```

Step 2: Analyze Response

```
☐ Got a valid response
☐ Response makes sense
☐ Token count returned
☐ No errors occurred

Response Quality: ☐ Poor ☐ Fair ☐ Good ☐ Excellent
```

Challenge Part B: Multi-Turn Conversation

Step 1: Build a Conversation

```
messages = [
  {"role": "system", "content": "You are a Python expert."},
  {"role": "user", "content": "What is a decorator in Python?"}
]

# First turn
```

```
response1 = client.chat.completions.create(
    model="kimi-k1.5",
    messages=messages
)

# Add assistant response to conversation
messages.append({
    "role": "assistant",
    "content": response1.choices[0].message.content
})

# Second turn
messages.append({
    "role": "user",
    "content": "Can you give me a code example?"
})

response2 = client.chat.completions.create(
    model="kimi-k1.5",
    messages=messages
)

print("First response:")
print(response1.choices[0].message.content)
print("\nSecond response:")
print(response2.choices[0].message.content)
```

Step 2: Analyze

☐ Both responses made sense
☐ Second response built on first
☐ Context maintained
☐ Conversation flowed naturally

Multi-turn Quality: ☐ Poor ☐ Fair ☐ Good ☐ Excellent

Challenge Part C: Streaming Response

Step 1: Implement Streaming

```
response = client.chat.completions.create(
    model="kimi-k1.5",
    messages=[
        {"role": "user", "content": "Write a haiku about programming"}
    ],
    stream=True
)

print("Streaming response:")
for chunk in response:
    if chunk.choices[0].delta.content:
        print(chunk.choices[0].delta.content, end="", flush=True)

print()  # Newline
```

Step 2: Evaluate

☐ Text appeared in real-time
☐ Complete response received
☐ Worked smoothly

Streaming Experience: ☐ Poor ☐ Fair ☐ Good ☐ Excellent

Key Takeaways

- ☑ Request structure is straightforward and well-defined
- ☑ Message roles determine conversation flow
- ☑ Parameters control response characteristics
- ☑ Streaming enables real-time output
- ☑ Always handle errors gracefully
- ☑ Monitor token usage for cost control
- ☑ Maintain message history for multi-turn conversations

CHAPTER 13

Token Management & Cost Optimization

MODULE 3.3 • TIER 3: DEVELOPER INTEGRATION (ADVANCED)

Learning Objective

By the end of this module, you will understand:

- Accurate token counting for planning
- Cost calculation and tracking
- Optimization techniques for reducing costs
- Budget management strategies
- Monitoring and analytics

3.3.1 Token Counting Accuracy

Using Tiktoken

```
import tiktoken

# Get encoder for Kimi (uses GPT-4 encoding)
encoding = tiktoken.encoding_for_model("gpt-4")

# Count tokens in text
text = "Hello, how are you today?"
tokens = encoding.encode(text)
token_count = len(tokens)
print(f"Tokens: {token_count}")

# Decode tokens back to text
decoded = encoding.decode(tokens)
print(f"Decoded: {decoded}")
```

Counting Message Tokens

```
def count_message_tokens(messages, model="gpt-4"):
  """Count tokens needed for messages"""
  encoding = tiktoken.encoding_for_model(model)

  total = 0

  # Add tokens per message overhead
```

```
    # (Each message adds ~4 tokens for formatting)
    total += 4 * len(messages)

    # Count content tokens
    for message in messages:
        if isinstance(message["content"], str):
            total += len(encoding.encode(message["content"]))
        elif isinstance(message["content"], list):
            # For multimodal (images, etc.)
            for item in message["content"]:
                if item["type"] == "text":
                    total += len(encoding.encode(item["text"]))
                elif item["type"] == "image_url":
                    # Image tokens depend on resolution
                    # Approximate: 400-800 tokens
                    total += 600

    return total

# Usage
messages = [
    {"role": "system", "content": "You are helpful."},
    {"role": "user", "content": "Explain quantum computing"}
]

token_estimate = count_message_tokens(messages)
print(f"Estimated tokens: {token_estimate}")
```

Estimating Response Tokens

```
def estimate_total_tokens(messages, estimated_response=500):
    """Estimate total tokens for request"""
    prompt_tokens = count_message_tokens(messages)

    # Add response tokens
    total = prompt_tokens + estimated_response

    return prompt_tokens, estimated_response, total

# Usage
prompt_tokens, response_tokens, total = estimate_total_tokens(
    messages,
    estimated_response=1000
)

print(f"Input tokens: {prompt_tokens}")
print(f"Output tokens (estimated): {response_tokens}")
print(f"Total: {total}")
```

3.3.2 Cost Calculation

Understanding Pricing

```
PRICING STRUCTURE:

Input tokens:  $0.0006 per 1M tokens ($0.0000006 per token)
Output tokens: $0.0018 per 1M tokens ($0.0000018 per token)

Example:
├─ 10,000 input tokens: $0.006
```

```
├─ 5,000 output tokens: $0.009
└─ Total: $0.015

(Check Moonshot documentation for current pricing)
```

Cost Tracking

```python
class TokenCostTracker:
    def __init__(self, input_cost=0.0000006, output_cost=0.0000018):
        self.input_cost = input_cost
        self.output_cost = output_cost
        self.total_cost = 0.0
        self.total_tokens = 0
        self.requests = []

    def add_request(self, response):
        """Track a completed request"""
        input_tokens = response.usage.prompt_tokens
        output_tokens = response.usage.completion_tokens

        cost = (input_tokens * self.input_cost +
                output_tokens * self.output_cost)

        self.total_cost += cost
        self.total_tokens += response.usage.total_tokens

        self.requests.append({
            "input": input_tokens,
            "output": output_tokens,
            "cost": cost
        })

        return cost

    def get_stats(self):
        """Get usage statistics"""
        return {
            "total_requests": len(self.requests),
            "total_tokens": self.total_tokens,
            "total_cost": self.total_cost,
            "avg_tokens_per_request": (
                self.total_tokens / len(self.requests)
                if self.requests else 0
            ),
            "avg_cost_per_request": (
                self.total_cost / len(self.requests)
                if self.requests else 0
            )
        }

# Usage
tracker = TokenCostTracker()

response = client.chat.completions.create(...)
cost = tracker.add_request(response)

print(f"This request cost: ${cost:.6f}")
print(f"Stats: {tracker.get_stats()}")
```

3.3.3 Cost Optimization Techniques

Technique 1: Prompt Optimization

```
# ✗ Wasteful: Including unnecessary context
messages = [
  {"role": "user", "content": """
    Here's a lot of background information that
    might not be relevant. The API endpoint at
    /users/profile returns the following data...
    [Long explanation]

    My question is: How do I call this endpoint?
  """}
]

# ✅ Optimized: Direct and specific
messages = [
  {"role": "system", "content": "You are an API expert."},
  {"role": "user", "content": "How do I call the /users/profile endpoint?"}
]

# Savings: ~50-70% fewer tokens for prompt
```

Technique 2: Response Length Control

```
# ✗ Unlimited: Response could be very long
response = client.chat.completions.create(
  model="kimi-k1.5",
  messages=[{"role": "user", "content": "Explain machine learning"}]
  # No max_tokens specified
)

# ✅ Optimized: Set appropriate limits
response = client.chat.completions.create(
  model="kimi-k1.5",
  messages=[{"role": "user", "content": "Explain machine learning briefly"}],
  max_tokens=500  # Limit output
)
```

Technique 3: Batching Requests

```
# ✗ Inefficient: Many individual requests
responses = []
for item in items:
  response = client.chat.completions.create(
    model="kimi-k1.5",
    messages=[{"role": "user", "content": f"Process: {item}"}]
  )
  responses.append(response)

# ✅ More efficient: Batch similar requests if possible
# Or use caching if making same request multiple times
```

Technique 4: System Prompt Efficiency

```
# ✕ Long system prompt
system_prompt = """
You are an expert Python developer with 20 years of experience.
You specialize in writing clean, efficient, well-documented code.
You always follow PEP 8 style guidelines. You think about edge cases.
You write comprehensive docstrings. You prefer clarity over cleverness.
...more and more instructions...
"""

# ✅ Concise system prompt
system_prompt = "You are an expert Python developer. Write clean, documented code following PEP 8."

# The system prompt is included in every request
# Shorter = Less tokens = Lower cost
```

3.3.4 Budget Management

Setting Budget Limits

```
class BudgetManager:
  def __init__(self, monthly_budget_dollars):
    self.budget = monthly_budget_dollars
    self.spent = 0.0
    self.requests = 0

  def can_make_request(self, estimated_cost):
    """Check if request is within budget"""
    return self.spent + estimated_cost <= self.budget

  def add_cost(self, cost):
    """Record a cost"""
    self.spent += cost
    self.requests += 1

    remaining = self.budget - self.spent
    percentage = (self.spent / self.budget) * 100

    print(f"Cost: ${cost:.6f}")
    print(f"Spent: ${self.spent:.2f} ({percentage:.1f}%)")
    print(f"Remaining: ${remaining:.2f}")

  def check_budget(self):
    """Check budget status"""
    if self.spent > self.budget * 0.8:
      print("WARNING: Used 80% of budget")
    if self.spent >= self.budget:
      print("ERROR: Budget exceeded!")

# Usage
budget = BudgetManager(100.0) # $100/month

estimated = count_message_tokens(messages) * 0.0000006 + 500 * 0.0000018

if budget.can_make_request(estimated):
  response = client.chat.completions.create(...)
  budget.add_cost(estimated)
else:
  print("Would exceed budget")
```

```
budget.check_budget()
```

Hands-On Challenge 3.3

Objective

Master token management and cost optimization.

Challenge Part A: Token Counting

Step 1: Count Tokens

```
import tiktoken

encoding = tiktoken.encoding_for_model("gpt-4")

test_texts = [
    "Hello, world!",
    "This is a longer sentence with more words.",
    "Machine learning is a subset of artificial intelligence..."
]

for text in test_texts:
    tokens = encoding.encode(text)
    print(f"'{text}' = {len(tokens)} tokens")
```

Step 2: Verify Estimates

```
Text 1: Your estimate: ____ Actual: ____
Text 2: Your estimate: ____ Actual: ____
Text 3: Your estimate: ____ Actual: ____

Accuracy of your estimation: ☐ Poor ☐ Fair ☐ Good ☐ Excellent
```

Challenge Part B: Cost Calculation

Step 1: Calculate Costs

```
# Make several API requests and track costs
tracker = TokenCostTracker()

messages_list = [
    [{"role": "user", "content": "Say hello"}],
    [{"role": "user", "content": "What is AI?"}],
    [{"role": "user", "content": "Explain quantum computing"}]
]

for messages in messages_list:
    response = client.chat.completions.create(
        model="kimi-k1.5",
        messages=messages
    )
    cost = tracker.add_request(response)
```

```
# Get statistics
stats = tracker.get_stats()
print(f"Total cost: ${stats['total_cost']:.6f}")
print(f"Avg cost per request: ${stats['avg_cost_per_request']:.6f}")
```

Step 2: Analyze

```
Total requests: ____
Total tokens: ____
Total cost: $____
Cost per request: $____
Cost per token: $____
```

Challenge Part C: Optimization

Step 1: Original Request

```
# Original - no optimization
response1 = client.chat.completions.create(
    model="kimi-k1.5",
    messages=[
        {"role": "system", "content": "You are an expert assistant. Please be thorough and detailed..."},
        {"role": "user", "content": "Explain Python decorators in detail with many examples"}
    ]
)

cost1 = (response1.usage.prompt_tokens * 0.0000006 +
        response1.usage.completion_tokens * 0.0000018)

print(f"Original cost: ${cost1:.6f}")
```

Step 2: Optimized Request

```
# Optimized
response2 = client.chat.completions.create(
    model="kimi-k1.5",
    messages=[
        {"role": "system", "content": "You are a Python expert."},
        {"role": "user", "content": "Briefly explain Python decorators"}
    ],
    max_tokens=500
)

cost2 = (response2.usage.prompt_tokens * 0.0000006 +
        response2.usage.completion_tokens * 0.0000018)

print(f"Optimized cost: ${cost2:.6f}")
print(f"Savings: {((cost1 - cost2) / cost1 * 100):.1f}%")
```

Step 3: Compare

```
Original cost: $____
Optimized cost: $____
Savings: ____ %

Original response quality: ☐ Poor ☐ Fair ☐ Good
Optimized response quality: ☐ Poor ☐ Fair ☐ Good

Was optimization worthwhile?
☐ Yes, good balance
```

☐ Somewhat, minor savings
☐ No, lost too much quality

Key Takeaways

- ☑ Use tiktoken for accurate token counting
- ☑ Understand pricing structure ($0.0000006 per input token)
- ☑ Track costs for all requests
- ☑ Optimize prompts without sacrificing quality
- ☑ Set max_tokens to control response length
- ☑ Implement budget management
- ☑ Monitor costs regularly

CHAPTER 14

Building Production-Ready Applications

MODULE 3.4 • TIER 3: DEVELOPER INTEGRATION (ADVANCED)

Learning Objective

By the end of this module, you will understand:

- Application architecture for Kimi integration
- Error handling and retry strategies
- Logging and monitoring
- Testing strategies
- Deployment best practices

3.4.1 Application Architecture

Recommended Structure

```
project/
├── src/
│   ├── client.py       # API client setup
│   ├── service.py      # Business logic
│   ├── models.py       # Data models
│   ├── config.py       # Configuration
│   └── utils.py        # Utilities
├── tests/
│   ├── test_service.py
│   ├── test_client.py
│   └── fixtures/
├── .env                # Environment variables
├── .gitignore          # Ignore .env, etc.
├── requirements.txt    # Dependencies
└── main.py             # Entry point
```

Client Wrapper

```
# src/client.py
import os
from openai import OpenAI, APIError

class KimiClient:
    def _init_(self):
```

```python
        self.client = OpenAI(
            api_key=os.getenv("MOONSHOT_API_KEY"),
            base_url="https://api.moonshot.cn/v1"
        )
        self.model = "kimi-k1.5"

    def create_message(self, messages, **kwargs):
        """Create a chat completion"""
        defaults = {
            "model": self.model,
            "temperature": 0.7,
            "max_tokens": 2000
        }
        defaults.update(kwargs)

        return self.client.chat.completions.create(
            messages=messages,
            **defaults
        )

    def create_message_stream(self, messages, **kwargs):
        """Create a streaming chat completion"""
        kwargs["stream"] = True
        return self.create_message(messages, **kwargs)

# Usage
client = KimiClient()
response = client.create_message([
    {"role": "user", "content": "Hello!"}
])
```

3.4.2 Error Handling

Comprehensive Error Handling

```python
# src/service.py
from openai import (
    APIError,
    APIConnectionError,
    RateLimitError,
    AuthenticationError,
    APIStatusError
)
import time
import logging

logger = logging.getLogger(__name__)

def make_request_with_retry(client, messages, max_retries=3):
    """Make API request with retry logic"""

    for attempt in range(max_retries):
        try:
            response = client.create_message(messages)
            return response

        except AuthenticationError as e:
            logger.error(f"Authentication failed: {e}")
            raise  # Don't retry auth errors

        except RateLimitError as e:
```

```
            if attempt < max_retries - 1:
                wait_time = min(2 ** attempt, 60)  # Exponential backoff
                logger.warning(f"Rate limited. Waiting {wait_time}s...")
                time.sleep(wait_time)
            else:
                logger.error("Rate limit exceeded after retries")
                raise

        except APIConnectionError as e:
            if attempt < max_retries - 1:
                logger.warning(f"Connection error, retrying...")
                time.sleep(1)
            else:
                logger.error("Connection failed after retries")
                raise

        except APIStatusError as e:
            logger.error(f"API error {e.status_code}: {e}")
            if e.status_code >= 500:
                if attempt < max_retries - 1:
                    time.sleep(2)
                else:
                    raise
            else:
                raise

        except APIError as e:
            logger.error(f"Unexpected API error: {e}")
            raise
```

3.4.3 Logging and Monitoring

Structured Logging

```
# src/utils.py
import logging
import json
from datetime import datetime

def setup_logging():
    """Configure logging"""
    formatter = logging.Formatter(
        '%(asctime)s - %(name)s - %(levelname)s - %(message)s'
    )

    # File handler
    file_handler = logging.FileHandler('app.log')
    file_handler.setFormatter(formatter)

    # Console handler
    console_handler = logging.StreamHandler()
    console_handler.setFormatter(formatter)

    # Root logger
    root_logger = logging.getLogger()
    root_logger.addHandler(file_handler)
    root_logger.addHandler(console_handler)
    root_logger.setLevel(logging.INFO)

def log_request(logger, messages, response):
    """Log API request details"""
```

```
    logger.info(json.dumps({
        "timestamp": datetime.now().isoformat(),
        "event": "api_request",
        "message_count": len(messages),
        "input_tokens": response.usage.prompt_tokens,
        "output_tokens": response.usage.completion_tokens,
        "total_tokens": response.usage.total_tokens,
        "model": response.model
    }))

# Usage in service
setup_logging()
logger = logging.getLogger(__name__)

response = make_request_with_retry(client, messages)
log_request(logger, messages, response)
```

3.4.4 Testing

Unit Tests

```
# tests/test_service.py
import unittest
from unittest.mock import Mock, patch
from src.service import make_request_with_retry

class TestService(unittest.TestCase):
    def setUp(self):
        self.mock_client = Mock()

    def test_successful_request(self):
        """Test successful API request"""
        mock_response = Mock()
        mock_response.choices = [Mock()]
        mock_response.choices[0].message.content = "Test response"

        self.mock_client.create_message.return_value = mock_response

        result = make_request_with_retry(
            self.mock_client,
            [{"role": "user", "content": "Test"}]
        )

        self.assertEqual(result, mock_response)

    @patch('time.sleep')  # Don't actually wait
    def test_retry_on_rate_limit(self, mock_sleep):
        """Test retry on rate limit"""
        from openai import RateLimitError

        mock_response = Mock()
        mock_response.choices = [Mock()]
        mock_response.choices[0].message.content = "Response"

        # First call fails, second succeeds
        self.mock_client.create_message.side_effect = [
            RateLimitError("Rate limited"),
            mock_response
        ]

        result = make_request_with_retry(self.mock_client, [])
```

```
        self.assertEqual(result, mock_response)
        mock_sleep.assert_called_once()

if __name__ == '__main__':
    unittest.main()
```

Integration Tests

```
# tests/test_integration.py
import unittest
import os
from src.client import KimiClient

class TestIntegration(unittest.TestCase):
    @classmethod
    def setUpClass(cls):
        # Skip if no API key
        if not os.getenv("MOONSHOT_API_KEY"):
            raise unittest.SkipTest("No API key available")
        cls.client = KimiClient()

    def test_simple_message(self):
        """Test simple message exchange"""
        response = self.client.create_message([
            {"role": "user", "content": "Say hello"}
        ])

        self.assertIsNotNone(response.choices[0].message.content)
        self.assertGreater(len(response.choices[0].message.content), 0)

    def test_streaming(self):
        """Test streaming response"""
        stream = self.client.create_message_stream([
            {"role": "user", "content": "Count to 5"}
        ])

        chunks_received = 0
        for chunk in stream:
            chunks_received += 1

        self.assertGreater(chunks_received, 0)
```

Hands-On Challenge 3.4

Objective

Build a production-ready application with Kimi.

Challenge Part A: Application Setup

Step 1: Create Project Structure

```
mkdir kimi-app
cd kimi-app
mkdir src tests
touch src/__init__.py src/client.py src/service.py
```

```
touch tests/__init__.py tests/test_service.py
touch .env .gitignore requirements.txt
```

Step 2: Set Up Dependencies

```
requirements.txt:
openai>=1.0.0
python-dotenv>=0.19.0

pip install -r requirements.txt
```

Step 3: Create Client Wrapper

```
# src/client.py
# (Implement KimiClient class from above)
```

Challenge Part B: Error Handling

Step 1: Implement Error Handling

```
# src/service.py
# (Implement make_request_with_retry function)
```

Step 2: Test Error Handling

```
# Create scenario that triggers rate limit
# Verify retry logic works
```

Challenge Part C: Create Main Application

Step 1: Build Simple Chatbot

```
# main.py
import sys
from src.client import KimiClient
from src.service import make_request_with_retry

def main():
  client = KimiClient()
  messages = []

  print("Chat with Kimi (type 'quit' to exit)")
  print("-" * 40)

  while True:
    user_input = input("You: ").strip()

    if user_input.lower() == 'quit':
      break

    messages.append({"role": "user", "content": user_input})

    try:
      response = make_request_with_retry(client, messages)
      assistant_message = response.choices[0].message.content

      messages.append({
        "role": "assistant",
        "content": assistant_message
      })
```

```
        print(f"Kimi: {assistant_message}")

    except Exception as e:
        print(f"Error: {e}")

if __name__ == "__main__":
    main()
```

Step 2: Test

```
python main.py
# Type: "Hello, what is Python?"
# Verify response
# Type: "quit" to exit
```

Challenge Part D: Verification

☐ Application starts without errors
☐ Can send messages to Kimi
☐ Receive responses
☐ Multi-turn conversations work
☐ Can exit cleanly

Application Status: ☐ Poor ☐ Fair ☐ Good ☐ Excellent

Key Takeaways

- ☑ Structure code for maintainability
- ☑ Implement comprehensive error handling
- ☑ Add retry logic with exponential backoff
- ☑ Log important events and errors
- ☑ Write tests for critical paths
- ☑ Verify error handling works correctly
- ☑ Test both happy path and error scenarios

CHAPTER 15

Advanced Integration & Optimization

MODULE 3.5 • TIER 3: DEVELOPER INTEGRATION (ADVANCED)

Learning Objective

By the end of this module, you will understand:

- Advanced caching strategies
- Performance optimization techniques
- Scaling applications
- Best practices for production
- Future-proofing your code

3.5.1 Caching Strategies

Request Caching

```
# src/cache.py
from functools import lru_cache
import hashlib
import json

class RequestCache:
    def _init_(self, max_size=100):
        self.cache = {}
        self.max_size = max_size

    def _make_key(self, messages):
        """Create cache key from messages"""
        messages_str = json.dumps(messages, sort_keys=True)
        return hashlib.md5(messages_str.encode()).hexdigest()

    def get(self, messages):
        """Get cached response if exists"""
        key = self._make_key(messages)
        return self.cache.get(key)

    def set(self, messages, response):
        """Cache a response"""
        if len(self.cache) >= self.max_size:
            # Remove oldest entry
            oldest_key = next(iter(self.cache))
            del self.cache[oldest_key]
```

```
        key = self._make_key(messages)
        self.cache[key] = response

    def clear(self):
        """Clear cache"""
        self.cache.clear()

# Usage in service
cache = RequestCache()

def get_response(client, messages):
    # Check cache first
    cached = cache.get(messages)
    if cached:
        logger.info("Cache hit")
        return cached

    # Make API request
    response = client.create_message(messages)

    # Cache result
    cache.set(messages, response)

    return response
```

3.5.2 Performance Optimization

Parallel Requests

```
# src/parallel.py
import asyncio
from openai import AsyncOpenAI
import os

async def make_parallel_requests(requests):
    """Make multiple requests in parallel"""
    client = AsyncOpenAI(
        api_key=os.getenv("MOONSHOT_API_KEY"),
        base_url="https://api.moonshot.cn/v1"
    )

    tasks = []
    for messages in requests:
        task = client.chat.completions.create(
            model="kimi-k1.5",
            messages=messages
        )
        tasks.append(task)

    responses = await asyncio.gather(*tasks)
    return responses

# Usage
async def main():
    requests = [
        [{"role": "user", "content": "What is AI?"}],
        [{"role": "user", "content": "What is ML?"}],
        [{"role": "user", "content": "What is DL?"}],
    ]
```

```python
    responses = await make_parallel_requests(requests)

    for response in responses:
        print(response.choices[0].message.content)

if __name__ == "__main__":
    asyncio.run(main())
```

3.5.3 Scaling Applications

Load Balancing

```python
# src/load_balancer.py
from enum import Enum
import random

class ModelStrategy(Enum):
    ROUND_ROBIN = "round_robin"
    RANDOM = "random"
    LEAST_LOADED = "least_loaded"

class LoadBalancer:
    def __init__(self, models=None, strategy=ModelStrategy.RANDOM):
        self.models = models or ["kimi-k1.5"]
        self.strategy = strategy
        self.current_index = 0
        self.load_counts = {model: 0 for model in self.models}

    def select_model(self):
        """Select next model based on strategy"""
        if self.strategy == ModelStrategy.ROUND_ROBIN:
            model = self.models[self.current_index]
            self.current_index = (self.current_index + 1) % len(self.models)
            return model

        elif self.strategy == ModelStrategy.RANDOM:
            return random.choice(self.models)

        elif self.strategy == ModelStrategy.LEAST_LOADED:
            return min(self.load_counts, key=self.load_counts.get)

    def record_request(self, model):
        """Record request for load tracking"""
        self.load_counts[model] += 1

# Usage
balancer = LoadBalancer(
    models=["kimi-k1.5"],
    strategy=ModelStrategy.LEAST_LOADED
)

selected_model = balancer.select_model()
```

3.5.4 Best Practices for Production

Configuration Management

```
# src/config.py
import os
from dataclasses import dataclass

@dataclass
class Config:
    api_key: str = os.getenv("MOONSHOT_API_KEY")
    api_url: str = "https://api.moonshot.cn/v1"
    model: str = "kimi-k1.5"
    temperature: float = 0.7
    max_tokens: int = 2000
    max_retries: int = 3
    retry_wait_base: int = 1
    log_level: str = os.getenv("LOG_LEVEL", "INFO")
    cache_enabled: bool = os.getenv("CACHE_ENABLED", "true").lower() == "true"
    cache_size: int = 100

    def validate(self):
        """Validate configuration"""
        if not self.api_key:
            raise ValueError("MOONSHOT_API_KEY not set")
        if self.temperature < 0 or self.temperature > 2:
            raise ValueError("temperature must be between 0 and 2")
        if self.max_tokens < 1:
            raise ValueError("max_tokens must be positive")

# Usage
config = Config()
config.validate()
```

Health Checks

```
# src/health.py
from datetime import datetime

class HealthChecker:
    def _init_(self, client):
        self.client = client
        self.last_check = None
        self.status = "unknown"

    def check(self):
        """Check API health"""
        try:
            models = self.client.client.models.list()
            self.status = "healthy"
            self.last_check = datetime.now()
            return True
        except Exception as e:
            self.status = f"unhealthy: {e}"
            self.last_check = datetime.now()
            return False

    def get_status(self):
        """Get current health status"""
        return {
            "status": self.status,
```

```python
        "last_check": self.last_check.isoformat() if self.last_check else None
    }

# Usage
health = HealthChecker(client)
if health.check():
    print("API is healthy")
else:
    print(f"API check failed: {health.get_status()}")
```

3.5.5 Monitoring and Analytics

Usage Analytics

```python
# src/analytics.py
from dataclasses import dataclass
from datetime import datetime, timedelta

@dataclass
class TokenStats:
    input_tokens: int = 0
    output_tokens: int = 0
    total_tokens: int = 0
    request_count: int = 0
    total_cost: float = 0.0
    start_time: datetime = None

    def add_response(self, response, input_cost=0.0000006, output_cost=0.0000018):
        """Add a response to stats"""
        self.input_tokens += response.usage.prompt_tokens
        self.output_tokens += response.usage.completion_tokens
        self.total_tokens += response.usage.total_tokens
        self.request_count += 1

        cost = (response.usage.prompt_tokens * input_cost +
               response.usage.completion_tokens * output_cost)
        self.total_cost += cost

    def get_report(self):
        """Generate usage report"""
        elapsed = datetime.now() - self.start_time if self.start_time else None

        return {
            "period": f"{self.start_time} - {datetime.now()}" if self.start_time else "N/A",
            "requests": self.request_count,
            "input_tokens": self.input_tokens,
            "output_tokens": self.output_tokens,
            "total_tokens": self.total_tokens,
            "total_cost": f"${self.total_cost:.4f}",
            "avg_cost_per_request": f"${self.total_cost / self.request_count:.6f}" if self.request_count > 0 else
"N/A",
            "avg_tokens_per_request": self.total_tokens // self.request_count if self.request_count > 0 else 0
        }

# Usage
stats = TokenStats(start_time=datetime.now())

# After each request
response = client.create_message(messages)
stats.add_response(response)
```

```
# Get report
report = stats.get_report()
print(report)
```

Hands-On Challenge 3.5

Objective

Implement advanced features and monitoring.

Challenge Part A: Add Caching

```
# Extend main application with caching
from src.cache import RequestCache

cache = RequestCache()

# Modify get_response to use cache
def get_response_cached(client, messages):
    cached = cache.get(messages)
    if cached:
        print("[CACHE HIT]")
        return cached

    print("[CACHE MISS - API CALL]")
    response = client.create_message(messages)
    cache.set(messages, response)
    return response
```

Test:

```
python main.py
# Ask same question twice
# Should see [CACHE HIT] second time
```

Challenge Part B: Add Analytics

```
# Add usage tracking
from src.analytics import TokenStats

stats = TokenStats(start_time=datetime.now())

# In main loop, after each response:
stats.add_response(response)

# At end of program:
print("\n" + "="*40)
print("SESSION STATISTICS")
print("="*40)
for key, value in stats.get_report().items():
    print(f"{key}: {value}")
```

Test:

```
python main.py
# Have 3-4 conversation turns
```

```
# Exit with 'quit'
# Should see usage report
```

Challenge Part C: Configuration

```
# Use Config class
from src.config import Config

config = Config()
config.validate()

# Use in client creation
client.model = config.model
client.client = OpenAI(
    api_key=config.api_key,
    base_url=config.api_url
)
```

Challenge D: Verification

```
✅ Caching works (cache hits on repeated questions)
✅ Analytics tracks usage
✅ Configuration loads from environment
✅ Application is scalable
✅ Production-ready

Application Features:
☐ Basic (just works)
☐ Intermediate (error handling + logging)
☐ Advanced (caching + analytics + config)
☐ Production-ready (all features)
```

Key Takeaways

- ✅ Implement caching to reduce API calls
- ✅ Use async for parallel requests
- ✅ Track usage for optimization
- ✅ Configure via environment variables
- ✅ Implement health checks
- ✅ Monitor and log important metrics
- ✅ Plan for scaling from the start

Tier 1 Appendices

APPENDIX A: GLOSSARY - TIER 1 TERMS

API (Application Programming Interface)

Technical interface allowing software programs to communicate. Kimi offers an OpenAI-compatible API for developers.

Context Window

Maximum amount of text (in tokens) that an AI model can process and maintain coherence across in a single conversation.

Hallucination

When AI generates plausible-sounding but false information. Common in all LLMs.

LLM (Large Language Model)

Artificial intelligence model trained on massive amounts of text to understand and generate human language.

Moonshot AI

Company that developed Kimi AI.

Token

Smallest unit of text processed by AI. Roughly 1 token ≈ 4 characters or 0.75 words.

File Parsing

Process by which Kimi analyzes and extracts content from uploaded files.

OCR (Optical Character Recognition)

Kimi's ability to read text from scanned PDFs and images.

Prompt Engineering

Art and science of crafting inputs to AI systems to produce desired outputs.

APPENDIX B: QUICK REFERENCE - TIER 1

WHEN TO USE KIMI:
☑ Analyze multi-page documents
☑ Compare multiple files
☑ Extended conversations
☑ File parsing/understanding
☑ Complex problem-solving
☑ Strategic decision-making

TOKEN BUDGETING:
200K total tokens
Documents: 50-100K
Conversation: 100K+
Rule: 40% upload, 60% discussion

PROMPT FORMULA:
[Context] + [Task] + [Constraints] + [Format] = Success

CONVERSATION FLOW:
Setup (1) → Initial Response (1) → Refinement (2-4) →
Application (1-2) → Closure (1) = 6-10 messages typical

FILE UPLOADS:
☑ Upload: PDF, Code, Images, Spreadsheets, Docs
✕ Don't upload: Binary executables, encrypted files
💡 Size limit: Usually 100MB
Remember: Multiple files at once is possible

APPENDIX C: RECOMMENDED LEARNING PATH

WEEK 1: Foundations
└─ Complete modules 1.1-1.3
└─ Do all hands-on challenges
└─ Have 3-5 practice conversations

WEEK 2: Mastery
└─ Complete modules 1.4-1.5
└─ Use Kimi for real tasks
└─ Build your prompt library

WEEK 3+: Application
└─ Use Kimi regularly
└─ Expand to Tier 2 content
└─ Build expertise

Tier 2 Appendices

APPENDIX A: GLOSSARY - TIER 2 TERMS

Chain-of-Thought (CoT)

Prompting technique asking AI to explain reasoning step-by-step. Dramatically improves accuracy for complex problems.

Few-Shot Learning

Providing examples in prompt to demonstrate desired output format or behavior.

Hierarchical Querying

Building understanding progressively from general to specific using previous context.

Multimodal

Ability to process and understand multiple types of input (text, images, etc.) in the same conversation.

Hallucination

When AI generates plausible-sounding but false information.

Task Decomposition

Breaking complex problems into smaller, more manageable sub-tasks.

Token Budget

Planned allocation of available tokens to documents, conversation, and analysis.

Cross-Verification

Asking same question in different ways to verify answer consistency.

Source Attribution

Noting and citing where information came from to enable verification.

Confidence Calibration

Understanding when AI is appropriately confident vs. overconfident.

APPENDIX B: QUICK REFERENCE - TIER 2

```
WHEN TO USE CHAIN-OF-THOUGHT:
- Multi-step logic problems
- Strategic decisions
- Complex analysis
- Problem-solving requiring reasoning

WHEN TO USE FEW-SHOT:
- Subjective classification
- Style matching
- Format requirement
- Domain-specific output

WHEN TO DECOMPOSE TASKS:
- 5+ distinct components
- High importance of accuracy
- Need to verify each step
- Complex problem

LONG-CONTEXT STRATEGY:
1. Pre-process documents
2. Query hierarchically
3. Verify with citations
4. Synthesize findings

MULTIMODAL BEST PRACTICES:
- Only include relevant formats
- Make relationships explicit
- Ask format-specific questions
- Verify visual understanding

WEB SEARCH CHECKLIST:
☐ Need current information?
☐ Fact-checking claim?
☐ Need recent developments?
☐ Outside training data?

ERROR PREVENTION:
- Request sources for claims
- Cross-verify important answers
- Ask for reasoning explanation
- Test edge cases
- Check against known facts
```

Tier 3 Appendices

APPENDIX A: API REFERENCE QUICK GUIDE

```
ENDPOINTS:

Chat Completions:
POST https://api.moonshot.cn/v1/chat/completions
├─ model: "kimi-k1.5"
├─ messages: [...]
├─ temperature: 0-2
├─ max_tokens: integer
└─ stream: boolean

Models:
GET https://api.moonshot.cn/v1/models

STATUS CODES:
200: Success
400: Bad Request
401: Unauthorized (invalid API key)
429: Rate Limited
500: Server Error
```

APPENDIX B: ENVIRONMENT VARIABLES

```
MOONSHOT_API_KEY=sk_...
MOONSHOT_API_URL=https://api.moonshot.cn/v1
MOONSHOT_MODEL=kimi-k1.5
LOG_LEVEL=INFO
CACHE_ENABLED=true
MAX_RETRIES=3
```

APPENDIX C: COMMON ERROR SOLUTIONS

```
ERROR: AuthenticationError
SOLUTION: Check API key is set and valid

ERROR: RateLimitError
SOLUTION: Implement backoff retry logic

ERROR: Connection timeout
SOLUTION: Check network, implement retry

ERROR: max_tokens exceeded
SOLUTION: Reduce max_tokens or break into chunks
```

APPENDIX D: CODE TEMPLATES

Basic Request Template:

```
response = client.chat.completions.create(
  model="kimi-k1.5",
  messages=[
    {"role": "system", "content": "You are helpful."},
    {"role": "user", "content": "Question here"}
  ]
)
print(response.choices[0].message.content)
```

Streaming Template:

```
for chunk in client.chat.completions.create(
  model="kimi-k1.5",
  messages=[{"role": "user", "content": "Question"}],
  stream=True
):
  if chunk.choices[0].delta.content:
    print(chunk.choices[0].delta.content, end="", flush=True)
```

Error Handling Template:

```
try:
  response = client.chat.completions.create(...)
except RateLimitError:
  print("Rate limited")
except APIConnectionError:
  print("Connection error")
except Exception as e:
  print(f"Error: {e}")
```

www.ingramcontent.com/pod-product-compliance
Lightning Source LLC
LaVergne TN
LVHW041208061126
851857LV00018B/1983

* 9 7 8 9 7 7 9 5 6 8 7 4 4 *